THE UNITED STATES ARMY IN TRANSITION

SAGE SERIES ON ARMED FORCES AND SOCIETY

INTER-UNIVERSITY SEMINAR ON ARMED FORCES AND SOCIETY

Morris Janowitz, *University of Chicago*
  Chairman and Series Editor

Charles C. Moskos, Jr., *Northwestern University*
  Associate Chairman and Series Editor

Sam C. Sarkesian, *Loyola University*
  Executive Secretary

Also in this series:

THE UNITED STATES

ARMY IN TRANSITION

PREPARED BY INTER-UNIVERSITY SEMINAR ON ARMED FORCES AND SOCIETY

Zeb B. Bradford, Jr.

Frederic J. Brown

with a foreword by Sam C. Sarkesian

 SAGE PUBLICATIONS   Beverly Hills / London

The opinions, conclusions and recommendations of this manuscript do not represent the official position of the Department of Defense or any other agency of the United States government or the Woodrow Wilson International Center for Scholars. The views are strictly those of the authors. Permission to quote all or any part of this manuscript must be given by the authors, as well as the publishers (see below).

For information address:

SAGE PUBLICATIONS, INC.
275 South Beverly Drive
Beverly Hills, California 90212

SAGE PUBLICATIONS LTD
St George's House / 44 Hatton Garden
London EC1N 8ER

Printed in the United States of America

International Standard Book Number 0-8039-0211-5

Library of Congress Catalog Card No. 72-98029

FIRST PRINTING

To our wives
Inge and Anne

CONTENTS

IV: THE MILITARY PROFESSION IN A NEW ERA

FOREWORD

Whether one feels that the United States involvement in Vietnam was an aberration of our general policy or was in fact a sign of the future, one cannot help but wonder regarding its impact on the military establishment. It is perhaps too soon after the event to attempt definitive analyses; nevertheless, the U.S. military is faced with problems that crystallized during the Vietnam period, and perhaps because of it, require immediate response. The anti-military sentiments in society, a general decline of the prestige of the military, a growing restiveness within the professionals—all of these are issues which need to be faced now.

A new international environment is also evolving, partly as a result of the end of the U.S. ground role in Vietnam and partly as a result of the end of the Cold War mentality. In any case, this has added to the difficulties encountered by the U.S. military in adapting to the post-Vietnam era.

The end of the Vietnam War and the new international order have had some immediate impact on the military establishment—the all-volunteer military, for example. There are, of course, many others involving force postures, combat capability, weapons procurement, and security policy in general. A number of scholars have addressed these issues and continue to do so. But it is unusual to have regular military men seriously consider such matters in the public forum.

This book is written by two West Point graduates, both having served in Vietnam, and both having given serious consideration to the nature of the post-Vietnam military establishment. They have published articles in professional journals addressing the issues of the U.S. Army in Vietnam and its role in national security. Although all the services have similar problems, the U.S. Army has the greatest, perhaps because of its ground role, its involvement in overseas bases, and its past dependence on the selective service system. The authors, applying their academic background combined with professional experience, are able to integrate the theoretical with the practical and bring some useful and thought-provoking insights into the nature of the U.S. Army in transition during the post-Vietnam era. In so doing, they present a range of alternatives for dealing with the post-Vietnam period. Whether one agrees with their assessments and recommendations is not as important as recognizing that these are being presented by active regular Army officers—in itself a unique event. Their analyses, assessments, and conclusions regarding the U.S. involvement in Vietnam and the kinds of security policies and military establishment that should be developed reveal interesting insights into professional values and perceptions. The authors represent a new breed of army officers—those who are well grounded in intellectual processes and not afraid to articulate their assessments in these terms.

The publication of this volume has been undertaken by the Inter-University Seminar on Armed Forces and Society, not because of the specific content and views it contains. Rather it is felt that the volume represents a worthwhile contribution to the understanding and study of the role of the military in our society. The mode of analysis and the conclusions are not necessarily shared by the Fellows of the Inter-University Seminar. The Inter-University Seminar on Armed Forces and Society is composed of over three hundred social scientists with academic and scholarly commitments whose interests cover a wide range of subjects within the area of armed forces and society. The Fellows of the Inter-University Seminar hold a wide range of policy views but they are all concerned with intellectual and academic analysis of military institutions as they undergo change. In this respect the Inter-University Seminar provides a framework and focal point through which intellectual interchange can be fostered, research stimulated, and studies published.

—Sam C. Sarkesian
Chicago, Illinois
1973

PREFACE

This book concentrates upon ground power, and the institution which has historically been charged with the principal responsibility of leading and managing it, the United States Army. This focus is taken deliberately for two reasons. First, it is the dimension of military policy we know best. Second, it is a dimension of military power which is greatly affected by the transformation occurring in the world of today, and whose future is most uncertain. Much of what we say about the changing demands being placed upon national military policy and upon the Army applies to other forms of power and the other military services or to the Joint Chiefs of Staff or Office, Secretary of Defense. We leave those areas to others, hoping they will soon be explored. It is our belief that a responsible assessment of the multiple challenges confronting the chief instrument and organization of land warfare is sufficient for one book.

We hope to overcome three principal problems which we believe have plagued most attempts to deal with amending military policy. The first is an unfortunate compartmentalization of tactics and strategy. National security policies are castles of sand unless founded upon tactical military capabilities. Yet how often have we posited a strategy based upon perceived need, and then belatedly examined our capacities for implementing it? Or how often have we followed tactical doctrines in accordance with traditional practices, without

[13]

due attention to the larger implications such practices may have for policy?

The second failure is a compartmentalization of the demands of combat and the effective employment of forces on the one hand, and the realities of the military institution and the profession on the other. That these must be compatible is obvious to the point that no elaboration should be necessary, but for a variety of reasons the interrelationship has seldom been acknowledged sufficiently. We feel that the effectiveness of ground power is inextricably bound up with the professional and bureaucratic drives which motivate the commissioned and non-commissioned officer corps and which bear heavily on the extent to which the nation can or should place its trust in its armed forces.

The third and final shortcoming we will attempt to avoid is the perennial, and we think spurious, gap between the "requirements" approach which tends to view needs as somehow divorced from costs, and the equally simplistic "resources" approach which in pure form takes the resources on hand and buys what can be afforded, with insufficient consideration given to the fact that this may be totally out of line with what could be afforded were true needs properly communicated. Ends and means cannot be considered in isolation. Every individual knows this intuitively. When he shops for a house or an automobile, he automatically attempts to accommodate his needs to his pocketbook, and vice versa.

If we are successful in this attempt we will avoid these deficiencies. We hope that our perspective and experience as career military officers will assist us in this effort to suggest integrated solutions. We have initiated our study with an assessment of the evolving context of security policy, particularly as it affects ground power, in Part I. New conditions, experiences, attitudes, and constraints all interact to establish new parameters within which programs governing military power must be devised, and which prescribe appropriate roles for the military institution to play with regard to society. In Part II we outline means by which the Army may respond to the new demands of strategy imposed upon it. After establishing certain guidelines which take new conditions into account, we suggest a comprehensive new approach to the basic design and mission of Army forces. A model of a "Ready Army" demonstrates the organizational requirements of new strategic concepts and provides a vehicle by which the resource implications of these may be examined. In this part we also turn to several major substantive policy areas in which response is required if we are to meet new demands of national security. Three of these—Army support of NATO, Reserve Forces policies, and Army support of diplomacy—require adjustments in external orientation of Army programs. A fourth, capital intensification, is concerned more with new departures in practices internal to the Army which bear heavily on its ability to accommodate the conflicting pressures of expensive manpower and difficult missions. In all of these areas we deal primarily with Army combat forces and how they should be employed and improved.

A changing American society is also requiring parallel adjustments in the Army's institutional structure and practices. We deal with these in Part III, in two major aspects. One lies in adjusting the organization of the Army itself to a rapidly changing society. The other suggests the means by which Army resources may properly be used in support of the non-military goals of society.

The final chapters, in Part IV, deal with a difficult and sensitive area, but one which cannot be left unaddressed in any serious attempt to adjust to new conditions. We discuss a new professional ethos and the problem of the competence and integrity of the officer corps and what we feel are appropriate remedies.

We recognize the controversial nature of the subject matter of this book, and realize that some will strongly disagree with certain of our approaches. It should be clearly understood that our purpose in writing this study is not to advocate smaller forces or to seek cheaper security. It is rather to suggest some clearly defined alternatives to current policy which will assist the nation and the Army in adjusting to the demands of a new era. We hope that our ideas are accepted in that vein. We have written this book solely because of our dedication to the security of the nation, and to the profession of which we are part.

This book is the product of shared experiences and collaboration over an extended portion of our careers. It grew in part from a series of articles done for the *Military Review* in the February through June 1972 issues. It would not have been written without the inspiration, support, and assistance of many associates, both civilian and military, and of the institutions which they represent and serve. Indeed we are in the debt of so many that adequate acknowledgement of all who have helped us is simply not possible. But we do wish to express our gratitude in particular to certain sources of support without which this work would have been either much longer in coming or not done at all. The Inter-University Seminar on Armed Forces and Society directed by Morris Janowitz provided essential guidance and assistance to us in developing our ideas and in helping us to prepare the manuscript for publication. The Woodrow Wilson International Center for Scholars, directed by Benjamin H. Read, provided not only crucial administrative support and assistance but has over the period of the year of preparation of this work provided the opportunity and the forum for the development and discussion of many of the ideas herein. We also wish to thank the Army War College and the National War College for their encouragement and unstinting support for this effort, which was written during our association with those institutions. Finally, we wish to acknowledge the critical influence exerted by George A. Lincoln, William E. DePuy, and John W. Seigle who inspired us to address the larger issues and who provided an atmosphere conducive to honest and intensive analysis of the problems of our profession and our nation. While we are in the debt of all of these, the ideas presented are our own, for which we as individuals take full responsibility. They do not represent the position of the Department of Defense or any of the individuals or institutions mentioned above.

Part I

THE CHANGING CONTEXT OF

SECURITY POLICY

Chapter 1

FROM COLD WAR TO COALITION SECURITY

> *We face problems that no past generation has faced.*
> *They are common problems of humanity. Most great*
> *cultures developed independently. Now we are in close*
> *contact every day, yet it is a fact of our existence that*
> *we have never really assimilated. Yes, we must rethink*
> *where we are.*

> —Henry Kissinger

The composition and deployment of the United States Army must always be closely attuned to the way the nation perceives the international environment, how it defines the national interests within that environment, and how it prefers to protect those interests. For this reason, it is necessary as a first step to outline certain features of the emerging environment which have important implications for security policy—particularly for ground power. This is done to provide an appropriately broad context and basis for our more detailed suggestions concerning policy.

[21]

EROSION OF COLD WAR BLOCS

The approach to security which has guided our policies for a generation is becoming inappropriate for the conditions facing us in the future. The continued transformation of the international arena from a system of opposing ideological and military blocs toward one of greater diversity proceeds apace. This requires modification of a "containment" strategy based upon the assumption of a monolithic Communist threat and a corresponding American willingness and capacity to lead in countering it. It is of course possible, even perhaps a temptation, to overstate the erosion of Cold War conditions. This must be avoided.

The enormous strength of the two superpowers continues to exert a crucial influence on international affairs. Continued competition between them, even if apparently less volatile than at times in the past, remains a central element of the global status quo. Yet relationships among the major powers are, in general, becoming more dynamic. The United States, Western Europe (the European Community), Japan, China, and the Soviet Union appear to be developing divergent and to some extent non-ideological paths away from the blocs of the Cold War. Japan offers an example. Given impetus by unilateral U.S. trade policies, and movement toward a new policy vis-à-vis China, Japan is now simultaneously reassessing its relationships with Taiwan, China, and the Soviet Union. The new postures which are likely to result from this could bring into question the U.S. role as "protector" of Japan against an aggressive Communist bloc in spite of an enduring interest in a friendly and peaceful Japan. While Western Europe is a much different case, particularly in that we continue to have large ground forces there, relationships are nevertheless changing. West Germany's growing confidence in her ability to initiate a dialogue with the East over the future of Europe bears witness to a new questioning of Cold War assumptions. A larger and more truly European Common Market which will be the result of British and Scandinavian entry will add increasing economic power to a more confident European political voice.

Perhaps the single most significant alteration in Cold War alignments has been the gradual shift of the People's Republic of China out of the Soviet orbit. Inevitably this represents a move toward the United States at least in contrast to its previous relationships. But while this move has fragmented the Communist world, it has also introduced a major new dimension of uncertainty for all major world powers. Should this uncertainty continue, shifting alliances may characterize our world in the 1970s and 1980s as blocs characterized the world of the 1950s and 1960s. All of this indicates that while our objective will be a stable peace, our philosophy of security policy must be one of bargaining, hedging, and attempts to prevent unfavorable shifts in a more complex and fluid system. The environment may begin to resemble that of the nineteenth-century, pre-World-War-I era characterized by frequently changing military arrangements within the European balance of power system.

A COMPETITIVE ARENA

The principal powers within that arena (Britain, France, Russia, Prussia, and Austria) shared a common interest in preserving the system itself. National aspirations were legitimate only if they were compatible with the basic national interests of the other parties. Furthermore, no state alone had the power to dominate the remainder. States sought security from necessity through coalition arrangements, which would adjust to changing power relationships and interests. Underlying the system was the mutual recognition that accommodation, even between nations of differing ideologies (such as republican France and tsarist Russia) was essential to continuation of an acceptable status quo. While there are indeed vast differences between a nineteenth-century concert of Europe and our emerging world of the 1970s, there are nevertheless some parallel features, particularly when contrasted with the two-power, ideologically charged and uncompromising world of the Cold War of the early post-World-War-II period—the principal one being an acceptance that, while competition may be intense, all parties must accept compromise. Then, as now, distribution of power did not permit single-power dominance, yet isolation was not a feasible alternative. The fate of each nation was too closely bound up with others to permit a go-it-alone approach.

The somewhat similar situation which seems to be developing today is perhaps more difficult for the United States to accept than for other nations with different twentieth-century experiences. Until this century, broad oceans dominated by the British Navy permitted us the freedom to build a nation and tame a continent in isolation from most of the hard choices of international affairs which faced the powers of Europe. And until we entered World War I, we had not been an important factor in global politics. After that foray abroad, which we chose to view as righteous and unambiguous, we reverted to our tradition of non-involvement and avoidance of "foreign entanglements" in the interwar period. During and after our entry into World War II, we were in an enviable and unique position, which we have tended over time to accept as normal. We were in a position in which compromise was largely unnecessary and could be considered as unworthy of a morally righteous nation. We were in a position of dominance over our allies and uncompromising hostility with regard to our wartime enemies. Victory over the Axis did not really change the pattern. Domination over a wartime alliance was transferred to supremacy over a broader grouping of impoverished former allies and enemies in a Cold War alliance. Hostility to Hitlerism was replaced by ideological hostility to Communism. Accommodation was usually unnecessary with friends and considered both unnecessary and wrong with our foes. This outlook was perhaps comforting although it was not always reconcilable with the actual situation. We acknowledged the limits of our power to influence Soviet actions in Eastern Europe (especially in the case of the Hungarian uprising of 1956) and the victory of the Chinese Communists. But we found that our rhetoric impeded if not precluded any accommodation.

A significant feature of the current era is that the United States is coming to acknowledge, as it must, that it cannot simply choose between isolation or domination, even rhetorically. Our interests are too bound up with others to permit us to withdraw from the scene and trust to fate to preserve us. Yet we have neither the power nor the inclination to maintain a dominant position over our environment. The rhetoric, and to some extent the posture, of containment reflected the approach to national security and diplomacy of an era when we believed we still had the choice of being uncompromising. But in order to preserve our interests in a more ambiguous world, that approach is inadequate. It also appears beyond the means we can devote to the task if domestic demands on our resources are to be met.

The United States still possesses tremendous power which will enable it to continue to play a key role in the international arena, even as that arena becomes more unpredictable. By applying its power selectively in support of its interests on a pragmatic basis, the United States can insure that hostile powers, or groups of them, will not dominate the world scene either in terms of controlling vital land masses, resources, and peoples, or through comprehensive coalitions.

A hostile, bipolar world was grim indeed, but it was also

simple in that it served to underwrite a general consensus over the nature of the threat to our vital interests. This of course left room for disagreement over how this should be countered. Especially for the design of ground forces it offered a point of departure. In that context, the "front line" was easily definable and therefore provided an unambiguous means of establishing "requirements" for forces. This was therefore a useful world view for designers of Army forces. The principal contingencies—wars with the Communist world—were explicit. They were in a sense "announced." The question of the basic purpose of ground forces rarely had to be addressed.

While there are still important features of a bipolar environment still facing us, particularly in the strategic nuclear area, the ground has begun to shift. New approaches are needed; new concepts for the role of conventional power should be examined.

LEGACIES OF A CONTAINMENT APPROACH

A transformation of the international system away from some of the more rigid confrontation features of a bipolar Cold War era toward a more fluid, multipolar milieu complicates the search for new approaches. While alliance policy and military assistance has served many different purposes in addition to the comparatively narrow one of adding defensive combat capability to Cold War allies, that purpose has been primary and has been sufficient to provide an operative rationale for most programs. In simplistic terms, assistance has been seen essentially as fortifying the barriers defending our side of a fixed status quo. "Forward defense" nations—those which by their location were considered as most likely targets of Communist aggression—were the recipients of the bulk of military-assistance resources. Both in Europe and in Asia a "cordon sanitaire" of friendly regimes was the geopolitical reflection of a strategy of containment. This system cannot be said to have been either unsuccessful or unrealistic during much of the post-World-War-II era. But it has produced established patterns of relationships which now run counter to a desire for greater flexibility in some cases. Certain of these, such as our relationship with Taiwan, are undergoing re-examination as a result.

An eventual consequence of a geographic containment approach was the attempt to implement a strategy of "flexible response" in support of it. This was consistent with the view that Communist hostility was monolithic. All forms of aggression had to be countered, and it followed that a range of U.S. military capabilities to cover the spectrum of possibilities was prescribed. This has supported our continued large presence in Europe backed by a large reserve force. It has also led to our attempt to apply containment in insurgency situations, particularly in Southeast Asia. The conclusion that a containment approach is becoming inadequate does not imply that the approach was not appropriate when developed nor that it has been unsuccessful. Its inadequacy is perhaps due to the success of past American policy that has produced the world of diversity we have been dedicated to achieving. Nor does such a conclusion imply that a requirement for defense no longer exists. If anything, the post-containment era may be more unsettled, dangerous, and uncertain for our interests.

INVOLVEMENT ABROAD

Whether or not the Cold War changes its character or even disappears, the United States will have a strong, perhaps increasing, interest in maintaining a compatible international environment. Our fate is inextricably bound up in affairs abroad due to economic imperatives as well as to politico-military considerations.

With only 7% of the world's population the United States accounts for half of the world's raw-material consumption. Our dependence on foreign sources for these is growing rapidly. At the beginning of this century we were virtually self-sufficient in minerals, for example. But by 1970 some 22% of our required minerals were imported. By the end of this century we can expect that over half of our needed minerals must be imported should this rate of consumption continue (Figure 1-1).

Our growing dependence on foreign oil sources provides an important illustration not only of our involvement abroad but of how economic interests became bound up in international politics. The United States now obtains some 50% of its energy from petroleum and about 25% from natural gas

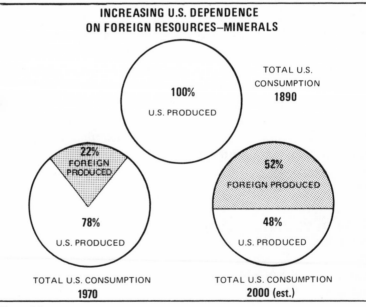

**INCREASING U.S. DEPENDENCE
ON FOREIGN RESOURCES—MINERALS**

100%
U.S. PRODUCED

TOTAL U.S.
CONSUMPTION
1890

22%
FOREIGN
PRODUCED

78%
U.S. PRODUCED

TOTAL U.S. CONSUMPTION
1970

52%
FOREIGN PRODUCED

48%
U.S. PRODUCED

TOTAL U.S. CONSUMPTION
2000 (est.)

Figure 1-1.

which is closely associated with petroleum. Our reserves of oil and gas are rapidly declining. George A. Lincoln, former Director of the Office of Emergency Preparedness, estimates that excess productive capacity will be essentially gone in two to five years. We are already less than self-sufficient in our basic energy resource and may face a critical situation by the middle of the decade.*

The United States is not the only advanced nation becoming increasingly dependent on foreign sources for basic energy. Japan is dependent upon the Middle East for all but 3% of its oil, which is only one of the many resources vital to the U.S. and others becoming scarce. We are proceeding into a world which is rapidly exhausting many resources essential to sustain life and industrial vitality. This will present us with some sobering choices. We will find ourselves increasingly reliant on other nations' willingness to provide strategic resources to us. Alternatively we must live within our own resources and moderate the demands which characterize our life style.

Another indication of our growing interests and involvement abroad lies in our rapidly expanding private investment around the world. During the decade of the 1960s our private investment in Europe grew over 200%, in the Middle East 60%, in Latin America 65%, in Canada 90%, in Africa almost 250%, and in Southeast Asia almost 200%. Here again the links between economic and political realities become apparent. There is no question that political stability is an essential precondition for the continued vitality of private

---

*Since the basic text was written, the importance of foreign sources of oil to the United States has been dramatically demonstrated by the actions taken by some of the oil producing states during and after the Middle East conflict of 1973.

investments abroad. The importance of these remaining viable has been increasingly clear as a counter to a deteriorating trade balance which has now joined an adverse balance of payments.

The U.S. share of earnings on direct investment abroad totaled almost $9 billion in 1970. This substantial capital return is a principal pillar of U.S. international economic strength. Politico-military stability is a key factor in the preservation of this favorable situation. In Europe, for example, where U.S. private investment is in excess of $20 billion, any alteration in U.S. military policy must take into account its likely effect upon the vital but intangible stability which underwrites our economic posture, in addition to any more narrowly military consideration in terms of a NATO-Warsaw-Pact balance. U.S. economic involvement abroad cannot be divorced from consideration of our national security in the future, even should containment itself become completely outdated.

Quite apart from economic considerations, the more obvious problems resulting from continued political competition and risk-taking of various powers will remain. A whole new range of uncertainties is being opened up as relationships between the larger powers continue to evolve. For example, there is no assurance that China and the Soviet Union will resolve their differences peacefully. Any open conflict between them could have far-reaching effects —extending to parts of the world where our interests and those of our allies are involved. We would need to have appropriate forces, as well as other means, to protect against the potential side-effects of such an occurrence.

COALITION SECURITY

These developments are cited to illustrate that U.S. interests in what happens abroad are likely to endure beyond containment, although continued concentration on "threat" as the sole justification for programs will fail to provide us with an adequate approach. We do not know how various national interests, ours and others, will be translated into policies, or under what ideological banners the political manifestations of them will march. But they will march, and we must proceed with caution into an unknowable future.

As the foregoing suggests, many of the "givens" of the past decades are changing and perhaps eroding, yet we in the Army may not have adjusted our thinking sufficiently to view the international environment in terms of our enduring interests as well as in terms of the Cold War military threats to which we have become accustomed.

We need to reshape our thinking in terms of two principal groups of powers, rather than continue to view the environment as divided into two well-defined and hostile armed camps. One group consists of those large powers such as the Soviet Union or Japan which can play an autonomous international role in either cooperation or competition with the United States. The other group is composed of lesser powers, such as South Korea, which tend to be viewed by the larger powers as peripheral in importance and which generally must react to developments generated by others. The Army will need to develop the insights and the flexibility to support the U.S. in its permanent quest for favorable relationships both with major powers who are simultaneously potential partners and competitors, and with smaller powers who may affect us in a variety of ways—by virtue of unique roles they may play, positions they occupy, resources they possess, or through commitments we have made to them. We must learn to move from a containment approach of unambiguous friends and enemies to one supporting "coalition security," in which our policies and forces are designed to cope with a more unpredictable environment. This is not a very convenient or comfortable basis for designing ground forces, especially in comparison to the relatively simple bipolar system of the previous two decades, for which containment was a reasonable response.

Adjusting to a coalition-security approach is an exceedingly difficult challenge for the military establishment. This will be especially so for the Army, whose strategy, forces, and institutional practices are part and parcel of a truly "seamless web" of capability. To change the strategic assumptions which underlie the deployment and configuration of ground forces would have extensive ramifications for virtually every aspect of Army policy—reserve as well as active elements. Today we have an Army primarily oriented on the assumptions developed during the Cold War era, with the principal generator of requirements and policies remaining the large-conventional-war contingency.

Subsequent chapters will deal with the particular adjustments to current policy which are required by the Army to respond to this challenge. At this point, however, it is useful to suggest a conceptual basis for assessing our forces and our posture in support of coalition security, in which we must retain deployable forces for a range of unannounced contingencies.

INSURANCE POLICY

Military forces ought to be considered premiums paid for accident insurance. The estimated risk of having an accident, and the penalty we are willing to accept if we have one, determines the size of the premium we are willing to pay.

The likely kinds of mishaps influence the form of protection we buy. Even the optimistic person buys some insurance if he is prudent. The difference, of course, is that forces, unlike insurance premiums, may actually change the degree of risk. But the analogy has enough validity to illustrate the basic rationale for deployable ground forces, as well as the difficulty of making precise determinations of how much is needed. This is by way of saying that beyond meeting current policy commitments one cannot *prove* the need for any particular level of ground forces, but that prudence dictates that we *ought* to retain them for unknown but probable future contingencies which will take place within an uncertain future political context. As opposed to the "announced" Cold War contingencies, this calls for a substantially different kind of military posture. It is important to remember that we are dealing with an unknown and essentially unknowable future and that therefore we must be guided by probabilities, not certainties. That the probabilities of various contingencies are changing with the continued transformation of the environment there can be no doubt. In a world of numerous competing powers, all constrained by power limitations and certain basic mutual interests, it seems clear that a variety of lesser contingencies, such as peacekeeping, limited local wars, and competition over resources will be elevated in comparison with the more serious major ones, such as strategic war and large-scale conventional war. Certainly, however, continuation of current commitments such as NATO remains of great importance.

The need is for a *reshaping* of our ground forces in order that we may proceed into the uncertain decade ahead with appropriate instruments of policy to meet these lesser contingencies. We should expect that the pattern which is likely is one of participation in various forms of coalitions to favorably influence the environment or to counter opposing powers who would influence it in a manner unfavorable to our enduring interests. But the means will be tailored to the ends sought. That is, limited ends characteristic of coalition security will tend to limit the policy instruments employed. The Army faces a range of difficult adjustments if it is to adequately support a coalition-security approach. The basis for planning will be more difficult in a world of increasing diversity. Understanding the new patterns of a shifting international milieu is a necessary precondition for the determination of new security policies. But alone this understanding is insufficient. New directions must also be consistent with the emerging constraints on the development and employment of ground power which flow from evolving domestic realities.

Chapter 2

EMERGING CONSTRAINTS ON

AMERICAN GROUND POWER

The transformation of the international milieu in progress is paralleled by equally important change in our domestic arena. The Army must adjust to this changing America if it is to be capable of serving it effectively. There are two major dimensions of change to which the Army must respond. One dimension encompasses the changing values, attitudes, and life style of individual Americans as we proceed toward a "post-industrial" society. A number of perceptive observers such as Daniel Bell and Zbigniew Brzezinski have described the evolution of individual values and mores. Changing attitudes toward authority, established institutions, and the traditional work ethic are but a few of the new challenges to the Army in a more pluralistic era. How the Army should meet these challenges through leadership and new institutional practices is in itself a complex problem to which much attention will be directed in later chapters.

At this point, however, we are concerned with another major dimension of social change. That is the impact of changing domestic constraints on the strategic capabilities of our military instruments, particularly of ground forces.

Changing public attitudes, based upon experiences and evolving values, and a range of other factors constitute new realities which must be taken into account in developing security policy for the future. It is important to realize that many of the more significant constraints which are developing are perhaps neither explicit nor intentional and may be the unanticipated or even unintended consequences of policies or conditions in other areas. A perceptive man skilled in the ways of large organization has said, "Show me your programs and I will tell you your policies." To a certain extent we must recognize that our actual strategic policies are often derived in just this way.

THE VIETNAM LEGACY

The Vietnam legacy looms like a mountain, casting a long shadow indeed over security policy, especially as it relates to ground forces. Our military involvement in South Vietnam endured longer than any other war in American history except the Revolutionary War itself. Only World War II has cost the United States more in financial resources. As to Americans killed in action the losses in Vietnam are comparable to those we suffered in World War I. An analysis of the military lessons of that conflict will be the subject of a later chapter. Here we are dealing with the more general effects of it on the shape of policies and popular attitudes.

One of the most important results of our long involvement in Vietnam is a keen public skepticism concerning the utility of ground power and a new awareness that its employment can have distinct disadvantages as well as advantages particularly in the political arena. Its introduction to a cause can involve and commit a nation far more deeply than perhaps intended initially. The recognition of this inherent characteristic of ground forces is not likely to be soon forgotten and will have marked effects on future security policy. Ground troops of a modern democracy possess this unique quality for two main reasons. First, once employed they commit the nation to protect the lives of the soldiers involved and to "redeem" them if lost. There is nothing new in this. In 1910, when asked what support from the British and French would be desired in the event of a German invasion, General Foch is said to have replied, "A single British soldier—and we will see to it that he is killed." Second, ground troops uniquely involve and commit a power because once introduced into a combat situation they cannot easily be extracted. While aircraft and ships can often reverse course and make a clean break, ground forces rarely can do so once engaged. For better or worse their employment burns the bridges of easy political or logistical withdrawal.

Substantial doubt has arisen over the wisdom of the strategy which seemed to prescribe our entry into the Vietnam conflict—flexible response. We have learned that in strategic terms ground power can be quite inflexible once committed, however much flexibility it may provide on a tactical level. This is in spite of the fact that it can serve to demonstrate a commitment more clearly than can anything else. In the final analysis, "flexible response" was flexible only in a certain limited sense as it applied to ground forces. It gave us only a one-way flexibility by providing a variety of means by which to commit ourselves and thus theoretically to provide deterrence across a broad spectrum of contingencies. But if and when deterrence failed, these were not matched by means enabling us satisfactorily either to use our force decisively or alternatively to decommit when a situation no longer required a continued effort or presence. Perhaps this latter case is an inevitable dilemma of any strategy for the employment of military power. If extraction from a situation is too easy, then the act of commitment itself becomes less significant. Nevertheless, the effect of our

TABLE 2-1

"Suppose there were a danger of a Communist takeover of (read list), would you favor or oppose U.S. military involvement, including the use of U.S. troops?"[a]

	% Favor	% Oppose	% Not Sure
Western Europe			
1973	42	44	14
1970	50	33	17
Japan			
1973	31	53	16
1969	39	21	40
Israel			
1973	31	52	17
1970	27	49	24
Thailand			
1973	23	60	17
1969	38	37	25

a. Washington Post, March 26, 1973

experiences is a strong public desire to avoid those situations in which we can become over-involved through the use of ground forces. This is reflected in Louis Harris polls published in 1969, 1970, and 1973 (see Table 2-1).

The drawbacks of opinion polls as guides to future public action are widely recognized. But certainly this striking opposition to the use of ground power abroad expressed in the poll indicates a substantial conditioner of military policy and must be taken into account in strategic planning.

VOLUNTEER FORCES

Largely in response to the Vietnam experience, there has developed a public policy of moving toward total reliance upon volunteer forces in the future. This has major implications for military strategy. For its effect will be to place much more formidable and explicit political constraints, in the form of manpower policies, on our ability to engage in sustained and intensive conventional warfare than we have experienced in a generation. Obviously this will not mean that the United States will lose the potential capability to conduct such warfare should it choose to do so. Strong popular support would permit this as it has in the past on many occasions. But such a capability will be clearly beyond the resources of smaller volunteer ground forces. Furthermore, the potential political constraints introduced by this manpower policy will have the effect of establishing a new threshold within the conventional spectrum of military contingencies—a threshold which has been less significant in the past and which has not adequately been taken into account by current strategic concepts. We have been able to assume for planning and force structuring purposes that there is a comparatively easy transition up the ladder of conventional conflict at least until a nuclear threshold is reached. This can no longer be assumed. This point is so important that the nature of the strategic implications of prospective manpower policies requires examination in some detail.

A large and steady flow of replacements is a prerequisite for a sustained war on any significant scale, as can be illustrated by our extended effort in Vietnam. In combination with the one-year tour and a policy of individual replacements, the draft enabled the United States to pursue a limited ground war for more than six years. Without the draft we would have been faced fairly early in the war with the choice of changing our strategy—by either expanding the war or avoiding combat—or getting out. This was the kind of choice faced eventually by the French in Indochina. Under constitutional provisions, conscripts could not be deployed outside metropolitan France. Therefore, their professional units had to fight the war largely with what they began it.

Eventually the combat effectiveness of these units began to suffer since insufficient unit and individual replacements were available.

This was in sharp contrast to our own experience in Southeast Asia. Since 1965 nearly two million American military personnel have served in Vietnam. Our casualties have been distributed over that large number, rather than over the much smaller number of people serving in Vietnam at any given time. As a result losses have been widely diffused, without being reflected in the progressive weakening of combat units. These units were largely unaffected by losses, since they were sustained at full strength by a constant flow of replacements. Whether or not this kind of policy is desirable, a volunteer system would probably preclude it. Certainly we should not assume that we can attract sufficient volunteers in wartime to replace large losses even in a popular war, especially if strong anti-war attitudes prevail.

Without a continuous draft, any extended ground conflict which volunteer forces could not successfully terminate before being rendered ineffective by casualties would require a key political decision to alter manpower policy: either to re-institute the draft (or to initiate large draft calls in a stand-by draft situation) or to mobilize the reserves. Yet the pressures against these decisions are inevitably great.

A request for draftees in a limited-war situation would indicate first that the volunteer forces bought at such great money and effort were for peacetime cadre purposes only. Yet many Americans would doubtless question this rationale, since at least one of the major reasons we are attempting to move to a volunteer force is precisely to avoid the drafting of Americans to fight, especially in a limited-war context. If in fact the nation is expected to continue to rely on the draft when a conflict situation develops, as it does today, a need for much greater education of the public to this fact is clearly indicated since this point is not being stressed in efforts to achieve all-volunteer forces.

It would also make it clear that the nation was being asked to embark upon a substantially new course, requiring perhaps the development of a new national consensus over policy goals. This may be entirely desirable, but the effect would probably be not only to avoid those situations which might risk sustained war but also to create pressures against necessary display of military capability in a crisis situation.

There will also be large constraints on the use of reserves, especially as they are presently constituted, in a limited-war situation, even though current policies emphasize their importance as active forces decline in size. Again, this is based upon what one considers the true purpose of volunteer forces to be. A consequence of achieving a volunteer force would be that active duty personnel reasonably can be considered to be performing their chosen role if they are committed to combat. Furthermore they would likely be far more professionally motivated and more proficient than reserve combat units. Even if the reserves are volunteers, they may be distinctly inferior in both their outlook and competence.

Should we then consider reserve combat units in an all-volunteer environment as fully comparable to active units? Currently the active forces are merely the tip of the iceberg, with mobilized reserve units being "add ons" to them in a mobilization situation. But until very recently both active and reserve forces were made up largely of the same kind of non-professional manpower, largely drafted or draft-motivated. It seems likely that with volunteer active forces the pressures against commiting the reserves in a limited-war combat role will greatly increase even if people are drafted into them, unless a much closer linkage between active and reserve elements can be developed to compensate for what appears to be an increasing divergence between them.

Even leaving qualitative and professional questions aside, recent experience indicates that building a substantial reserve with volunteers will be very difficult in the absence of a draft for active forces. In his annual statement for fiscal 1973 Secretary of Defense Melvin Laird described the dramatic drop in reserve enlistments which came on the heels of a draft lottery system. In the half-year from June through December 1971, the total strength of the reserve components dropped from over 5,000 above to around 45,000 below statutory minimums. Certainly some of these effects can probably be offset with improved pay and other actions. But this experience indicates that compensating for the deficiencies of volunteer active forces is not a simple matter of turning to a reserve option. A possible draft for the reserves has been discussed. This would not, however, dissipate the qualitative distinctions between active and reserves. Indeed it would seem likely to increase them since active forces would then be volunteers and the reserves would be unwilling draftees.

There is another potential implication of moving to volunteer forces. This is a possible attitudinal change on the part of much of the public which would accompany a move from draftee to professional forces. If indeed Army ground forces possess a unique capacity to commit the U.S. because American men are placed on the line, it seems reasonable to assume that if those men are regarded as professionals, they will be considered somewhat more expendable in pursuit of a diplomatic or strategic cause than would be citizen soldiers. It is conceivable that casualties suffered by a volunteer force would be more acceptable to the public as a whole than would casualties suffered by a drafted force and that the anticipation of a volunteer force sustaining losses would be less distasteful to the public. Therefore, in both the conduct and the deterrence of conventional conflict they would perhaps commit the nation's interests less deeply, although certainly there is a size threshhold beyond which this would not be true.

BUDGETARY CONSTRAINTS

Public attitudes and competing national priorities are translated into budgetary realities. These, of course, have a decisive influence on military capabilities and must influence strategic planning and force development. An extremely important consequence of changing priorities has been pressure to place a relatively fixed ceiling on military spending with the prior year being taken as a norm. When imposed on the dynamics of the Army manpower situation, this operates to constrain ground power capability, especially in terms of size. As a practical matter, the resource "pie" must be optimally balanced between the sophisticated equipment necessary to success on a modern battlefield and the highly qualified and technically proficient manpower which can fully exploit it. It would be pointless to expend scarce dollars on advanced equipment at the expense of personnel competent to use it. It would likewise make little sense to hire more personnel than could be adequately equipped.

The requirement to achieve the proper balance within limited resources tends to rule out large-scale land forces in the foreseeable future, for the demands of materiel modernization compete with manpower for the defense dollar. At the same time, the accelerating costs of manpower, associated largely with efforts to increase the numbers of volunteers, means that each dollar buys less manpower. Inflation adds to the pressure. To illustrate, the Army forces which we maintained in fiscal year 1969 would have cost us over $4 billion more during 1972 owing to the increased cost of military manpower alone. Similar "cost growth" problems exist in the other military services. Such increases create pressures to reduce reliance on manpower and to become more capital-intensive. This, by militating against large ground forces, further reinforces the influence of other factors which tend to limit our capabilities for sustained ground combat on a large scale.

Means by which the Army should react to escalating manpower costs through internal adjustments will be discussed later. At this point it is sufficient to note that the Army must spend about half of a comparatively fixed budget to meet personnel costs. Within current Army resources the economics of this situation thus rules out substantially larger ground forces.

NUCLEAR WEAPONS

The use of ground forces cannot be adequately assessed without reference to nuclear weapons—tactical ones in particular. Since, fortunately, these have not been used, we must suppose that utility of the actual nuclear weapon has changed relatively less than that of conventional power, although as a deterrent its credibility is inevitably diminished in a world of greater tolerance for diversity. Fewer and fewer foreign policy goals are seen to be worth dying for as individuals, let alone as nations. But nuclear power in support of limited goals is potentially too unlimited to be very credible. This of course is nothing new. These are the kinds of considerations which brought a strategy of flexible response into being in the first place. It was the desire to have alternatives to a nuclear response which prompted the buildup of conventional forces in the early 1960s. Efforts to reduce manpower costs without reducing combat power cannot simply reverse the trend and go back to greater reliance on nuclear forces. Nuclear weapons are now known not to have deterred limited conflict in Southeast Asia or in the Middle East, nor were they employed. That this would be the case was not known in 1960, when it was believed that conventional war would be approached with much greater trepidation. Now there is probably greater reluctance to pay a high price for a nuclear option, as well as perhaps less active concern over the inherent risk of escalation that non-nuclear conflict entails. Nevertheless, we could be moving unintentionally into a dangerous situation in which the early use of nuclear weapons might be seen as the sole means of compensating for the limitations of ground power in the event a crisis situation were to escalate rapidly and we were to find ourselves involved with ground forces or with other vital interests at stake.

The challenge is to devise a means by which a tactical nuclear option has credibility while reducing the risks inherent in its possession. Since nuclear power has credibility only where the stakes involved can be shown to be reasonably worth the risks inherent in its use, it must, to be useful as a policy instrument, be tied to a context which makes the commitment of the United States credible. If configured properly, ground forces not only play a key role in developing such a context, as they do now in Europe, but any conventional capability they possess provides an alternative to early use or threat of use of nuclear weapons.

A CIRCUMSCRIBED ROLE FOR
GROUND FORCES

The combined effects of these diverse factors—the Vietnam legacy, all-volunteer forces, budgetary pressures and nuclear considerations—raise important new questions concerning the future roles of American ground power. These relate both to changing public perceptions which impact on policy and to our actual military capabilities.

Throughout the post-World-War-II period we could assume

that the conceptual underpinnings of our conventional forces were wholly relevant and adequate to the probable tasks of those forces. Based upon experience we believed that ground power was a uniquely fungible national asset which was readily available for a whole range of contingencies, subject only to a public decision to initiate the mechanism of deployment and mobilization. Yet it is clear that today we need to carefully consider our actual circumstances and the effects on our military capabilities of developing the attitudes and programs just discussed.

Vietnam is leaving at least a temporary bias against the employment of American troops abroad. This extends even to their positioning overseas in peacetime. Yet our forward strategy largely depends on our willingness and ability to project ground power to foreign land masses—and to convince others of this willingness and ability.

Volunteer forces inevitably will limit our capacity for conducting large sustained operations without mobilization, yet volunteerism itself appears to raise questions concerning the viability of our reserves as presently constituted and thus about mobilization as a reliable strategy.

Tight budgets combined with escalating manpower costs —largely produced by the attempt to raise a volunteer force—further militate against large forces and promote a search for technical means to offset expensive manpower. This again tends to bring into question our potential for rapidly translating large hypothetical assets into a large land army should that be required.

Evolving attitudes toward nuclear weapons seem likely to increase the risks associated with a "hostage" role for forward deployed forces, especially in light of potential problems in reinforcing them. Ground forces employed in the contest of a conventional arena must be better designed to cope with the actuality of a nuclear battlefield rather than acting as a mere trigger.

These factors are all closely related and help to form the

context of current security policy making. Guidelines for the development and use of ground forces which are consistent with these diverse factors are essential to realistic security planning for the 1970s. These must also take into account the crucial military lessons of Vietnam as they apply to Army forces, to which we now turn.

Chapter 3

THE LESSONS OF THE

VIETNAM EXPERIENCE

Realistic military policies for the future must take into account the impact of the Vietnam experience. Yet while we need to absorb the military lessons of that difficult conflict as they bear upon our capabilities, the contention and discord over our *goals* in Vietnam often tends to inhibit an honest appraisal of the *means* employed in support of policy. This has been particularly true with regard to the ground war, which has been viewed principally in terms either of scandalous vignettes or of dramatic operations such as the foray into Cambodia and Laos. General public understanding of the more typical operational features remains obscure. Deceptively simple terms such as "search and destroy" or "search and clear" explain little about the actual tactical employment of our forces, which was far from simple.

In order to evaluate our tactics in Vietnam, we must assess them against the situation facing our forces on the ground when we entered the conflict in force—both from our own point of view and from that of the enemy. His view was consistent with his previous experiences, convictions, and doctrines.

COMMUNIST MILITARY DOCTRINE

From the point of view of the enemy, success in conventional battle was essential to winning the war in South Vietnam. The Communists, at least initially, did not believe that success in guerrilla war could by itself lead to victory. They entered the conflict in South Vietnam with a formula for victory which had been tried and tested successfully against the French and had resulted in a stunning victory on the battlefield, culminating in the fall of the French fortress of Dien Bien Phu in 1954. This formula identified three main phases of conflict: "guerrilla war," "local war," and finally "mobile war."

Theoretically these phases run sequentially, with each phase paving the way for the one to follow. Actually, all of these phases have existed concurrently within South Vietnam, varying from place to place. The geographic compartmentalization and the primitive communications of Vietnam have contributed to this. The result has been a conflict in Vietnam which has been a virtual kaleidoscope of apparently unrelated actions, bewildering to many observers.

There is an enduring interdependence between these phases which remains throughout the course of a struggle. The organizational apparatus necessary for each phase is a key fixture of the succeeding one as well. For example, the local infrastructure constructed in the guerrilla war stage of the movement is needed to secure and maintain lines of communication and provide logistics support for the local war and the mobile war operations which occur later. In fact, a unique feature of Communist operations in Vietnam has been that military lines of communications are placed in front of the attacking main force—laid out in advance by the guerrilla war infrastructure and local war guerrilla forces. But also to be noted is the fact that because of this organizational depth the theoretically sequential phases are to some extent reversible. Conflict can be de-escalated by the insurgent high command when necessary, to a lower and perhaps less risky phase, provided the struggle has not seriously weakened the political apparatus. This helps to explain the resilience and persistence of the insurgent movement in Vietnam.

Reversion to a lower profile is, however, a temporary expedient to the insurgents, according to classical doctrine. Final victory requires successful progression to mobile warfare. Seizure of political power lies beyond the grasp of a movement which cannot prosecute conventional battle as a prelude to seizure of the reins of government. All activities which go before are necessary but insufficient ingredients. The willingness of Hanoi to suffer repeated disasters on the conventional battlefield against American main force units cannot be explained without reference to this doctrine.

A succinct description of the Viet Minh scenario for victory over the French and of the enduring philosophy motivating the Communist forces was given by General Giap in early 1950 (Fall, 1964: 34, 35):

> Our strategy early in the course of the third stage is that of a general counter-offensive. We shall attack without cease until final victory, until we have swept the enemy forces from Indochina. During the first and second stage, we have gnawed away at enemy forces; now we must destroy them. All military activities of the third stage must tend to the same simple aim—the total destruction of French forces.

> When we shall have reached the third stage, the following tactical principle will be applied: mobile warfare will become the principle activity, positional warfare and guerrilla warfare will become secondary.

There is room for argument over whether or not this abbreviated version of Giap's formulation encompassed the Communist approach in all its complexity. But there can be no doubt that enemy actions and troop deployments have been consistent with this conceptual approach. No more dramatic demonstration of the importance placed upon conventional success can be imagined than the massive invasion of South Vietnam by virtually the entire North Vietnamese Army in overt conventional fashion in April of 1972.

THE CONVENTIONAL NATURE OF THE WAR

The very large conventional component of the war is shown by Figure 3-1 which makes a comparison over time of opposing maneuver battalions. While there were always important features of guerrilla warfare present, from the time the United States entered in force in 1965 until the aftermath of the 1968 Tet offensive the war in South Vietnam was primarily one of big units fighting each other.

Prior to the intervention of U.S. ground combat forces in 1965 the Communist high command clearly sensed victory in South Vietnam. A long period of Communist preparation and chronic South Vietnamese political instability was now to be culminated with a straightforward defeat of the Army of the Republic of South Vietnam (ARVN). To execute the final stages of the campaign Hanoi deployed a large number of large units into South Vietnam beginning in late 1964. Some eight regiments were infiltrated into the south in 1965, joining a large number of Viet Cong units already present or being formed within South Vietnam. By mid-1965 the Communists could field considerably more maneuver battalions than could the ARVN. It was at this point that the U.S. entered in force. The conflict had therefore already reached its final stages, as far as Hanoi was concerned, when the U.S. intervened and began its buildup of regular forces. The ARVN was at the point of collapse, losing a battalion a week in the early months of 1965. Our escalation of forces

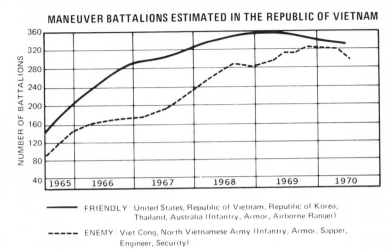

MANEUVER BATTALIONS ESTIMATED IN THE REPUBLIC OF VIETNAM

——————— FRIENDLY: United States, Republic of Vietnam, Republic of Korea,
Thailand, Australia (Infantry, Armor, Airborne Ranger)

- - - - - ENEMY: Viet Cong, North Vietnamese Army (Infantry, Armor, Sapper,
Engineer, Security)

SOURCE: Commander in Chief, Pacific; and Commander, US Military
Assistance Command, Vietnam, *Report on the War in Vietnam as of 30
June 1968*, US Government Printing Office, Washington, D.C.; and Joint
Chiefs of Staff, *Action Officer's Data Book on Vietnamizing the War.*

Figure 3-1.

was matched by Hanoi for an extended period, as Figure 3-1
clearly illustrates. In 1966 some fifteen more Communist
regiments were infiltrated into or formed within South
Vietnam. Therefore, contrary to widespread American public
misconceptions about the nature of the war, the task faced
by U.S. forces upon arriving in Vietnam was not one mainly
of tracking down guerrillas but of defeating an enemy field
army on the threshhold of victory.

Our units initially used more or less conventional tactics
because they had to in order to hold off disaster. In the
spring and summer of 1965 our forces served chiefly in a
reaction role, to assist South Vietnamese units being attacked. It was some time before we could move against the
enemy in his own base areas within South Vietnam. But by
the spring of 1966 this was possible; large unit warfare
continued, but with the U.S. forces on the offensive. After

having taken heavy losses, the enemy was forced to reassess his entire approach to the war. He could not get at the vitals of South Vietnam—the populated areas—without exposing his large units to disastrous defeat by U.S. firepower. Yet if he stayed in his secure sanctuaries, his local forces and infrastructure could neither be reinforced nor protected from increasingly active Vietnamese forces. By the end of 1966 the enemy had withdrawn most of his main force units into relatively secure base areas or cross-border sanctuaries, and the war within South Vietnam reverted to a lower level of conflict mostly involving small-scale fighting. Both U.S. and South Vietnamese forces were relatively free during this period to devote their attention to attempting to neutralize local forces and the Communist infrastructure. The summer and fall of 1967 were a comparatively quiet time in South Vietnam. The enemy had virtually vanished from the battlefield. This was the calm before the storm of the Tet offensive of 1968.

While the Tet offensive was an historic turning point in the war, and may in the perspective of history be viewed as a psychological success for the Communists, it did not produce what they planned and hoped it would in the short run—a general uprising of the people, large-scale disintegration of ARVN, and dramatic defeat of U.S. units. Instead staggering losses were suffered by both Viet Cong and North Vietnamese units and by the political infrastructure which had surfaced to support them in taking the cities.

The Tet offensive may well have been the beginning of wisdom for both the United States and Hanoi with regard to the nature of the war and their own respective limitations. Certainly we had not envisioned such ambition and capability by an enemy who had virtually none of the technical resources of modern war. On his part the enemy apparently put aside his hope for victory against U.S. ground forces on the pattern of Dien Bien Phu. From the Tet offensive until spring 1972, when Vietnamization was tested by massive conventional attack, the war changed in character. It became increasingly that of small unit actions and devolved to a far greater extent to South Vietnamese local forces as U.S. forces withdrew under the Vietnamization program. We may correctly say, then, that the large unit stage of the war was over after mid-1968—at least as far as the U.S. ground forces were concerned—and that the United States had innovated tactical means which successfully thwarted the original Phase III military goals of the enemy during that period. The scope of this analysis is limited to that earlier period.

COMPARISON OF ENGAGEMENTS

We succeeded against Communist main force units in a tactical arena where the French had failed. The reasons for our success can best be illustrated by comparing two engagements which occurred in different eras of the Vietnam conflict. One is drawn from the closing days of the French campaign against the Viet Minh, the other from the American experience in South Vietnam against the Viet Cong. The actions contain enough basic similarities to permit an analysis of some of their details. In both, the opposing forces were attempting to exploit their inherent advantages and both sides were seeking combat.

The first action, remembered as the battle of Mang Yang Pass, occurred near Pleiku in the Central Highlands in the early part of 1954. In an effort to gain tactical superiority over the Viet Minh, the French had reorganized many of their best combat units into "Group Mobiles". These elite task forces were designed to maximize mobility and heavy firepower to offset the advantages of cross-country mobility and flexibility possessed in abundance by the guerrilla forces. The force in this action was Group Mobile 100, formed in

November of 1953 and dispatched to the highlands in December to prevent Communist control of the area. Further north the historic battle of Dien Bien Phu was beginning to take shape. History has therefore cast the men of Group Mobile 100 and their opponents into the shadows of the greater battle.

For the first few months of 1954 Group Mobile 100 was in almost continuous movement throughout the highlands attempting to counter Viet Minh attacks on widely dispersed French strongholds. On April 1 it was ordered to An Khe to assume the defense of this vital sector endangered by Communist reinforcements.

The task force had already suffered 25% casualties from repeated contacts with the enemy by late June when it was ordered to evacuate An Khe and fall back to Pleiku—the key center in the highlands. Dien Bein Phu had fallen on May 8. The Group started on the eighty-kilometer road march on June 24. As a viable combat unit the force never completed the move.

Group Mobile 100 consisted of about 2,600 men at the time of the battle. Its basic combat units were three veteran French infantry battalions. These were the famed 1st and 2nd Korean Battalions, which had served under the United Nations flag with great distinction prior to coming to Indochina, and the Bataillon de Marche (B.M.) of the 43rd Colonial Infantry. A Vietnamese infantry battalion, the 520th, was attached. Accompanying these units was a formidable array of firepower in support—three battalions of 105 millimeter artillery of the 10th Colonial Artillery Regiment, the 3rd Squadron of the 5th Armored Cavalry, an armored car platoon, and limited air support on call from the French field at Nha Trang. Group Mobile 100 was fully mounted on wheeled or tracked vehicles—no one had to walk.

The enemy this potent force was destined to oppose was the 803rd Vietminh Regiment, manned at about the same strength. It was made up of four light infantry battalions and its fire support consisted only of 60 and 81 millimeter mortars and an unknown number of handheld rockets. It had no vehicles of any type, either tracked or wheeled, no artillery support and, needless to say, no air support. One would assume from comparing these forces in terms of equipment and weaponry that any engagement would be heavily in favor of the French. Yet Group Mobile 100 was virtually annihilated by the 803rd Regiment on its eighty-kilometer road march in the highlands.

As the French task force moved along Highway 19 from An Khe toward Pleiku in late June, it was ambushed by elements of the 803rd only fifteen kilometers outside of An Khe. Pinned down on the road and trapped amidst the wreckage of its own burning vehicles, Group Mobile 100 lost all of its artillery, almost all of its vehicles, and half of its men. The Viet Minh had attacked the column from the front and rear, making movement impossible for the French. They then destroyed the Frenchmen trapped on the road. The survivors lived by abandoning their equipment and taking to the jungle in small groups. A schematic picture of the disaster is shown in Figure 3-2.

The best that military technology could then provide had not been enough for the French. The mobility and firepower marshalled at such great effort had been rendered impotent in the face of a skillful but lightly armed foe. All that remains today of Group Mobile 100 is a simple marker in the Mang Yang Pass. The 803rd Viet Minh Regiment had turned the tide in the highlands. In the words of Bernard Fall: "This was the moment they had been waiting for, the battle which was going to repay them for hundreds of their own dead, and which was going to give them control of the plateau area" (Fall, 1964: 213).

More will be said about this vignette from the earlier stage of the Indochina war after a brief look at another operation which took place some twelve years later—the battle of Minh

THE BATTLE OF MANG YANG PASS

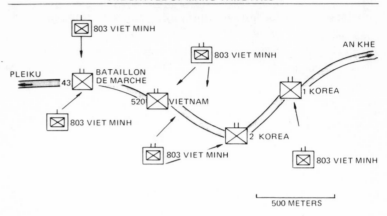

Figure 3-2.

Thanh Road in South Vietnam. This action took place in the dense jungle area north of Saigon, several kilometers northeast of the vast Michelin rubber plantation. The opposing forces this time were American and Viet Cong. On the American side was the 1st Brigade of the 1st Infantry Division. Their enemy was the 272nd Viet Cong Regiment. Employed eventually by the 1st Division were four infantry battalions and an armored cavalry squadron. These units were supported by five batteries of artillery and, significantly, by some sixty troop lift assault helicopters and massive air support both from helicopter gunships and fighter/bombers.

In this action, a successful effort was made by the Americans to entice the enemy into exposing himself by attacking our forces in a situation which on the surface appeared similar to that which had spelled the end of Group Mobile 100. This was done by the simple expedient of preparing a bogus convoy plan and insuring that it was leaked to the Viet Cong. At 0700 on the morning of July 9, 1966, an armored column departed Quan Loi bound for Minh Thanh, some twenty-five kilometers away along a narrow dirt road through the jungles of War Zone C. This column was comprised of most of an armored cavalry squadron (1st Squadron, 4th Cavalry) with its tanks and heavy firepower. At 1110 hours the 272nd VC Regiment attacked, immediately inflicting a number of casualties on the U.S. column. Here the similarity with the Mang Yang Pass affair ended. Within minutes reinforcing battalions of infantry were enroute by helicopter from 1st Division bases to attack the Viet Cong from his flanks and rear and to block his escape. The Commander of the 1st Division maneuvered four airmobile infantry battalions, airlifted from bases from ten to twenty kilometers distant from the scene of initial combat, to encircle the enemy. What had begun, as far as the Viet Cong were concerned, as a carefully prepared ambush turned into a larger-scale counter-ambush—a "vertical ambush" by air. Once pinpointed and fixed in position the 272d Regiment was hit by nearly one hundred air strikes over a period of several hours, as well as by continuous ground and artillery fire. It is estimated that about half of the 272d Regiment died in this holocaust, as compared to some twenty-four Americans. A sketch of the battle is in Figure 3-3.

These two engagements are taken as examples not because they had a large impact on the outcome of the war but because they are typical of the kind of combat which had evolved during the French campaign in Indochina in the 1950s and of that developed in South Vietnam more than a decade later. In the interim a key factor had been altered by technology, for which Communist military doctrine had no answer—the rate of reinforcement of committed forces. In the battle of Mang Yang Pass the French entered the fight with a given force. That force had to be sufficient to prevail against the enemy on its own, for it could not be assisted once committed deep in guerrilla-dominated terrain. The enemy selected and prepared the battlefield. Once the battle was joined, the initiative remained with the more lightly armed

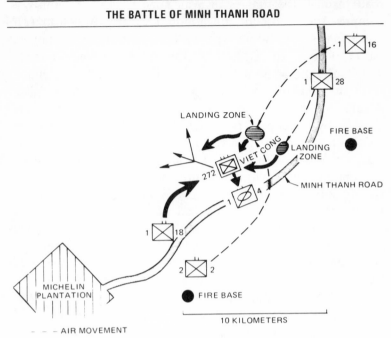

THE BATTLE OF MINH THANH ROAD

SOURCE: Developed from: Headquarters 1st Infantry Division, "After Action Report Operation *El Paso* II/III 2 June-3 September 1966."

Figure 3-3.

Viet Minh troops who could traverse the jungled battle area with speed and safety. The French vehicles, which provided high-speed mobility on the roads, became major encumbrances and highly vulnerable when stopped and exposed to a concealed enemy. Group Mobile 100 represented the ultimate in technology for its day. Its failure therefore led Bernard Fall (1964: 243) to conclude that only a guerrilla could defeat a guerrilla:

In the monsoon jungles of Southeast Asia, there is no cheap substitute for the most expensive commodity of them all—the well-trained combat infantryman; not the mass-produced item of the "divisional training camps" so dear to the Korean war, but the patiently trained jungle fighter who will stay in the jungle—not on the edges of it—and who will out-stay the enemy, if need be. The French had finally recognized this and their commando groups, once developed, showed surprising staying and hitting ability. But when the showdown came, there were too few of them—and they were too late.

More recently he has been echoed by a vocal critic of our efforts in Vietnam, Colonel David Hackworth (1968):

The most important lesson to be drawn from the war in Vietnam is that a lightly equipped, poorly supplied guerrilla army cannot easily be defeated by the world's most powerful and sophisticated army, using conventional tactics. To defeat the guerrilla, we must become guerrillas. Every insurgent tactic must be copied and employed against the insurgent. . .,. American forces must enter the guerrilla's lair as hunters, employing skill, stealth, enterprise and cunning.

These may have been appropriate conclusions for 1954 but not for today. The innovations illustrated by the Minh Thanh battle had come to characterize American combat operations against main force units by the time of the Tet offensive of 1968. These innovations rendered Hanoi's strategic approach inadequate. Technology has radically changed the dynamics of the battlefield.

With the helicopters available to him, given the distance of his bases from the battle, the American commander at Minh Thanh Road could reinforce at a rate of about twenty men every minute, or with the combat elements of almost an entire battalion every thirty minutes. Furthermore, these reinforcements did not have to stay in one place. Throughout the battle, units were frequently moved by air to block enemy escape routes and to complete his encirclement. There was no intention of conducting the battle with initially committed forces. Those were only used as the so-called price of admission.

This operation also illustrates a remarkable alteration in the traditional relationships between assault forces, particularly the infantry, and the supporting forces or weapons, especially the artillery. The traditional form of ground combat has required that infantry troops actually close with and destroy the enemy in direct fighting—wresting key terrain from him. Artillery and air strikes were clearly secondary in this effort, being used to soften up an enemy for the assaulting troops.

This relationship came to be reversed in Vietnam. To a large degree, the role of the infantry became primarily to locate and pin down the enemy in order that the coup de grace might be delivered by massive application of firepower from aircraft and artillery. This was the case in the Minh Thanh Road battle.

The role of armor as a mobile striking force was also altered in battles such as this one. Here the armor was used as a holding force, while more mobile infantry moved to outflank the enemy. This is a marked change from traditional employment.

In terms of our values and resources these role transformations were logical and sensible developments, for they reduced the exposure of our troops to the enemy. The last fifty yards to the enemy positions has been the grim province of the assaulting infantryman since the beginning of military history, and all too frequently the scene of his death. Airmobile tactics combined with heavy firepower has meant that that last fifty yards frequently did not have to be crossed. From a purely technical standpoint, frontal assault by the infantry fails to exploit our own assets. Our great wealth and production capacity have enabled us to provide an almost incredible amount of fire support to the foot soldier in Vietnam.

This has meant that our casualties in most large engagements in Vietnam have been substantially lighter than those suffered by the enemy. While obviously the North Vietnamese and Viet Cong have been willing to expend man-power and may have a large reservoir of able-bodied men, raw manpower alone does not constitute an army. It takes far longer to build an effective rifle battalion than to train a rifleman. Losses of the magnitude sustained by the Com-munists during the periods of Phase III battles must inevitably affect the quality of the enemy forces as a whole.

The alteration in the roles of supporting and assault forces constituted a serious derogation of enemy capability—one which he had not been able to foresee. The backbone of the insurgent movement in Vietnam has from the beginning been the superbly trained and motivated infantryman. But the airmobile warfare we have developed did not often permit him to be brought to bear in a direct contest with his opposite numbers—the American GI—on a conventional battlefield. There is an ironic similarity here. Many Western military leaders have decried the difficulty at "getting at" the enemy. Yet the enemy has found it even more difficult to "get at" our soldiers.

It is possible that Hanoi and the Viet Cong were wrong about the prerequisites for ultimate political success. It may be that they have on their part overestimated the require-ment for a military prelude to victory and underestimated the social and political momentum generated by a sustained level of violence. Certainly both sides entered the war with serious misconceptions. But it is fair to say that we have contrived a means of coping with the enemy when he seeks a conventional victory. We have done this in a way which, while very expensive in materiel, has compensated for some of the inherent defects of a largely draftee Western Army.

LESSONS FOR THE FUTURE

If our costly involvement in Vietnam is to be more than a painful memory, we must learn from it as we go about the task of building for the future. This discussion indicates that a significant conclusion to be drawn from Vietnam is that we successfully developed capabilities to operate effectively at the near-conventional stage. It is in this area that we should look for guidelines for future development of Army programs and doctrine, not in attempting to build a better counter-guerrilla capability as some would suggest. The principal challenge is to determine what is transferable to a conventional-type environment rather than to determine how we would do better next time in a future Vietnam-type situation.

Indeed, large-scale guerrilla or counter-guerrilla operations are poor options for our use in the future because of characteristics inherent in both insurgency warfare and in ourselves—no matter how much we would wish it otherwise. As the previous discussion should indicate, the contest in Phases I and II is at least as much social and political as it is military. At issue is political power—at the local as well as the national level. It is extremely difficult or even impossible for outsiders, especially foreigners, to operate with facility in this milieu. Precise and deep knowledge of local customs is essential. Acceptance by the local population is required, as is the ability virtually to "go native" in order to defeat the guerrilla on his own terms and in his own territory. It seems obvious that the U.S. Army is inherently ill-suited for producing substantial numbers of soldiers with these attributes. As an Army we are broadly representative of the general population—technically inclined, conditioned to a high standard of living, and—of greater significance—Western, largely white, and English-speaking. Only with great difficulty can many of our soldiers who are drawn from that population be given more than superficial training of the type needed to make them effective. Certainly our Special Forces personnel performed magnificently in Vietnam, but their example merely illustrates the point that a great deal of time and effort are needed to produce a competent guerrilla leader. And it is of course true that while the indigenous efforts were important, they were decidely subsidiary to the overall main force effort.

This is no reflection on our competence—merely an honest appraisal of our characteristics. There is no doubt that our citizens would themselves make superb guerrilla fighters if they were faced with a foreign force occupying the United States. But assisting someone else, of a different culture, to conduct internal politico-military battles amongst the population is an entirely different affair.

Added to these problems are thorny policy dilemmas caused by the dynamics of a revolutionary movement. A long period of Phase I and II activity precedes the escalation to conventional conflict. In order to be employed at an appropriately early point in a given insurgency situation, counter-guerrilla forces should be introduced long before overt hostilities develop. As a policy problem this presents immense difficulties. Assuming that we would wish to help defeat an insurgency in its early stages, how do we know which incipient movement, of many throughout the world, carries within it the germ of growth and potential ultimate victory? Would we not be faced with the prospect of almost always being either too late in the right place, or in the wrong place altogether? Even if we could correctly identify a truly dangerous movement, would it be possible to mobilize domestic support for an active U.S. role prior to the outbreak of highly visible Phase III operations? Finally, there is the problem of uniqueness. If there is anything students of revolutionary conflict agree upon (and there is not much) it is that generalization is dangerous. Each insurgency builds upon local issues and retains unique local characteristics.

How, then, is one to prepare a counter-guerrilla force for effective general employment? Would we have a group specifically targeted on each country or locale where a movement might develop? The alternative would be equally impractical—a group or a small number of groups trained for use in many areas, for this again confronts the problem of uniqueness. It would assume that general doctrine concerning counter-guerrilla operations can be developed to train large numbers of people for use in a variety of different places.

There is another even more complex problem associated with developing a significant counter-insurgency capability. This is the appropriateness of counter-insurgency as a major mission for the American Army itself. The great strength of American fighting forces historically has been precisely that they have exploited their uniquely American qualities and attributes. Highly mechanized and technical warfare reinforces our tendencies and talents and serves as a vehicle for evolutionary advance; counter-insurgency goes against the grain. We are a rich, industrial, urban country. Highly technical forces are compatible with our characteristics and resources.

Finally, technical conventional forces are likely to be most easily adaptable for general and rapid employment in an advanced conflict. This is important because we will in all likelihood be committed at the eleventh hour in any future conflicts, as we have been in the past. Therefore, we should design forces which can be committed with some chance of being effective in a mobile situation on short notice. Even should we become involved in insurgency-type situations, it is not likely to be at the inception of such a conflict. We are most probably going to be called upon as a fire brigade —placed in action after a fire is in its advanced stages, as we were in Vietnam. At that point, units designed for fighting guerrillas would be too little and too late, as they would have been in 1954 and 1965. This is one of the things we should learn—not that we must condition ourselves to become guerrillas.

The innovations which came about as a result of Vietnam must be productively employed by the Army in a range of different circumstances in support of coalition security—both in enhancing the capability of our own forces through appropriate capital intensification, and in assisting allies.

It can be—and has been—argued that what has been described here as a major tactical innovation in Vietnam merely illustrates the futility of the whole effort in Southeast Asia. It is pointed out, with some justification, that concentrating on defeating Phase III concedes the perhaps more important earlier phases to the insurgents. However, in a sense all military operations are in extremis—conducted as a last resort of the policy-maker. In Vietnam as elsewhere we did and indeed must place primary reliance in the early stages upon indigenous forces. If they cannot deal effectively with these activities, then probably we cannot either. But this does not negate our capability of blunting the victory in its mobile war stages. In other words, there is a residual capability of not losing if the enemy pursues Phase III doctrine. There is thus a dilemma for both ourselves and an insurgent force in a Vietnam-type situation—there is a ceiling on his effectiveness; there is a floor on ours. He can't win fighting our way, we can't defeat him fighting his way. Can he win ultimately if he limits his efforts to those activities associated with Phases I and II? We cannot answer this question from the Vietnam experience. For in the early years of our involvement the enemy chose not to conduct the war in that way, and of course the full judgment of history must wait until all the returns are in.

BROADER FEATURES OF THE WAR

This analysis is by no means an attempt to argue that what we have gained or learned in Vietnam has been worth its cost in lives, dollars, and domestic discord. Indeed, it is clear that some Americans at this time do not believe that it has been. But we must be careful that the perspectives of our future decision-makers are not formed by wrong or incomplete conclusions about Vietnam. We cannot tell what the future holds for us. Vietnam did more than demonstrate to us dramatically the limits of certain of our policies; it is also revealed rather clearly some of our inherent military weaknesses and strengths. We must know ourselves well enough to build upon our strengths and avoid our weaknesses in the future. It seems clear that Vietnam suggests a downgrading of the counter-insurgency option and a concerted effort to capitalize upon the advanced organizational and technical developments which it produced in the conventional areas.

There are a number of broader features of the Vietnam experience which should bear considerably on future policy. This analysis of ground power in Vietnam has not dealt with the crucial role of air or sea power. Both were vital to the kind of effort the Army made. Our strategic lines of communication were primarily protected by our naval forces. Our tactical lines of communications within South Vietnam were primarily by air, with Air Force fixed-wing aircraft providing absolutely essential support. This enabled ground forces to devote their efforts to the tactical mission, without large resources applied to securing and maintaining secure supply routes. Lastly, air and sea power have provided the crucial support to the Vietnamese Army which permitted the success of Vietnamization in the 1972 offensive.

Likewise, the Army tactics described here were made possible in large degree because of air superiority which permitted large helicopter formations and open movement on the ground, and also because of massive close tactical air support. Freedom of movement was restricted only by the enemy, terrain, and our own mobility assets, not by enemy air power or even the threat of it.

To a remarkable extent, therefore, the Army effort was dependent on the other services—a fact which tends to be forgotten. It should not be. Army effectiveness in the future will if anything be more dependent on integrated inter-service operations. The degree to which this integration was successfully achieved in Vietnam was due to great strides in command and control procedures and technical developments, principally in communications. American ground power was projected, sustained, and protected thousands of miles from the United States for a period of years. The efforts and resources necessary for this cannot be taken for granted in developing strategic concepts for the future.

Public discontent with the purposes to which the Army's efforts are applied in time inevitably come to include frustration and discontent with the Army itself. If the discontent is deep enough and lasts long enough, this can affect the tactical and thus strategic capabilities of the ground forces. It is hard to assess the true impact on unit morale and combat efficiency of concern over the Army's role in Vietnam.

Termination of a large ground effort makes it possible to avoid the issue as a practical matter. Yet we know the effect of public support, or lack of it, is crucial and must be considered in the future. Vietnam has given the Army a new awareness of its public nature. As noted in Chapter 2, we cannot divorce ourselves from the public policy we are to implement. This may very well further limit the employment of Army forces in high risk contingencies, where popular support is perhaps fragile or awaits vindication by demonstrated success.

Part II

RESPONDING TO EXTERNAL CHANGE

Chapter 4

SHAPING GROUND FORCES FOR

COALITION SECURITY

NATIONAL STRATEGY AND
ARMY POSTURE

The preceding chapters suggest a broad array of considerations which ought to guide future ground force development. There are formidable constraints both on the ends to
which ground power should be applied and on the means by
which it may be employed. Additionally there are inherent
limitations imposed by changing conditions under which
ground forces are to be raised, chief among these in
importance being a move to voluntarism. It is important to
keep in mind, however, that these important impacts on the
Army are not usually the result of deliberate public decisions
about the Army per se but are derived from public consensus
over other issues. For example, increased reluctance to
commit ground power abroad is produced by changing

AUTHORS' NOTE: We are indebted to the comment and counsel of Claude L.
Clark in the development of Ready Army roles and missions in coalition security
operations.

[73]

perceptions of national interests, not by explicit desires to limit the Army's role. As a servant of public policy, the Army must accommodate itself to the emerging mix of new conditions and realistically seek to find its place in support of national security strategy.

This has always been so. The Army's history is one of change, of contraction, expansion, and reorganization. As shown in Figure 4-1 the Army has been in constant flux since World War II. While there are many contributory sources of this constant change, the principle one has been the evolving approach to national security over the years.

The evolution of national strategy since World War II has been the subject of unending study and controversy. Ultimately, of course, basic domestic values and priorities play the pre-eminent role in determining the shape of national security policy by defining national interests.

THE ARMY'S CHANGING SIZE

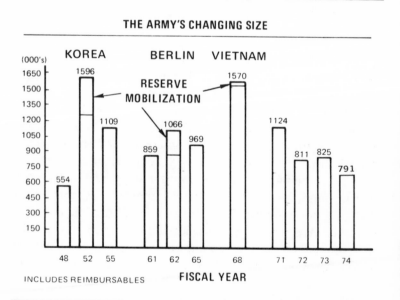

Figure 4-1.

After the frustrating experience of the Korean War, the United States by the mid 1950s had chosen to rely principally upon a nuclear deterrent to Communist attempts to upset a bipolar status quo. General purpose forces were accordingly reduced, and by the end of the decade the strength of the Army was substantially less than 900,000. While Army divisions were stationed in Europe and Asia in substantial numbers, U.S. declaratory strategy continued to rely primarily upon the specter of nuclear response to aggression. Ground forces were considered useful mainly in lending credibility to the general nuclear strategy.

The 1960s saw a dramatic reappraisal of the role of ground forces and general purpose forces across the board. A strategy of flexible response prescribed a broad spectrum of U.S. military capabilities to respond to, and hopefully therefore to deter, all levels of Communist aggression. Possible aggression was assumed to include nuclear aggression and blackmail as principal threats, but flexible response raised the priority of general purpose forces as the vehicle to counter other levels of conflict—unconventional and limited war. A credible flexible response was predicated upon maintenance of a large active Army establishment and the will to commit that establishment to combat.

Adoption of flexible response required acceptance of several key assumptions. In addition to postulating a somewhat mechanistic model of continuing and predictable bipolar confrontation, it also assumed possession of a broad range of actual military capabilities. Ability to achieve our goals in a counter-insurgency situation was one of the more significant capabilities which we assumed flexible response provided. But here the concept of non-nuclear deterrence played a cruel trick. Once a given capability was assumed by the political leadership, it was then assumed that deterrence had been achieved more or less by definition. Therefore, the potential costs and difficulty of living up to the rhetoric of deterrence, were it to fail, received less attention than they should have. After all, if possession of continuing successful deterrent capacity is assumed, the costs of exercising the capability become somewhat moot. Nevertheless, the active Army was increased substantially to almost 1,000,000 men by 1965. At the height of the Vietnam War commitment in 1968, it reached a peak strength of over one and one-half million. An important feature of that expansion was the absence of any substantial reserve augmentation, in contrast to the Korean War or the Berlin Wall crisis of 1962. The Army mobilized primarily from within its own resources.

The post-Vietnam reduction in Army strength is dramatic and is projected to reduce the Army to slightly over 790,000 by mid-1974. Personnel strength alone is an insufficient guide to Army capability. An equally relevant indicator is the number of divisions and how they are deployed. Shown in Table 4-1 is the divisional strength which corresponds to the strategies mentioned during representative years.

Of paramount importance is that although the Army is to be substantially smaller, we are implicitly projecting a set of flexible-response assumptions concerning our interests and military capabilities into a post-Vietnam future. The Army posture, which is presumably designed to implement a continuation of a flexible-response approach to containment,

TABLE 4-1

	1961	1968	1972
Military Strategy	Massive retaliation	Flexible response	Flexible response
Active Army Size	967,000	1,535,000	811,000
Active Army Divisions			
Europe	5	4	4
Asia	2	9 (7 RVN)	1
U.S.	9	5	8
Total	16	18	13
Reserve Divisions	37	8	8
Grand Total	53	26	21

SOURCE: IISS, *The Military Balance,* appropriate years. Excludes separate Army Reserve component brigades and Marine Corps units.

is less even than that military capability which we maintained during an era of so-called massive retaliation in the late fifties and early sixties when we relied on our strategic nuclear capability to deter all levels of conflict. Some adjustment seems required.

Under previous strategy high priority was given to maintaining a ready capability to enter into sustained conventional war. In strategies assuming the necessity of readiness to fight both 1½ and 2½ major conflicts simultaneously (1½ and 2½ war strategies), this large land warfare contingency centered on NATO-dominated strategic planning. In fact the NATO priority contingency mission became the justification for the vast bulk of Army forces.

THE SEAMLESS WEB OF
ARMY FORCE DEVELOPMENT

To a remarkable degree, the size and shape of the Army are closely linked to and have been responsive traditionally to near-term strategic assumptions such as NATO forward defense. The impulse for this linkage derives from the manpower-intensive nature of ground power. Therefore it is both expensive to maintain and is emphemeral. Immediate budgetary savings can be realized when a ground force unit is deactivated or reduced. The linkage also springs from our traditional insistence upon the presence of an agreed "clear and present danger" as justification for standing forces of any magnitude. This condition has a major influence on the Army's response to changing power relationships. Of greater importance at this transitional period in our history, the need for obvious, imminent "threats" inhibits the Army's ability to make reasonable adjustments to new realities in the absence of new threat assumptions which have been explicitly accepted by the political leadership. We call this complex linkage the "seamless web" of strategy and structure. Its effects bear detailed examination.

In the event of a general war, the majority of combat units of the active Army are planned to reinforce the forward deployed units according to a detailed scenario. The European contingency actually governs deployments in that for a general war contingency in NATO, Europe has priority over a comparable Asian contingency. This means that Army forces throughout the world must retain the capability for large-scale conventional war employment in Europe. The reserve forces are organized, equipped, and trained to follow up the active forces into the active theatre. The implications of this orientation extend, understandably, into the institutional fabric of the Army—its service school curriculum, officer corps organization, and much of the operating base structure. All must be capable of supporting a large mobilization and deployment under a World-War-II-type general war contingency.

All features of the Army are therefore largely subsumed under the strategic requirement of being prepared to fight a large continental land war. This means that proposals for substantial modifications of force levels—either of "forward deployed" units in Europe or across the board—are inconsistent with the Army's mission unless a corresponding restatement of our strategy is also suggested. As a result, proposals for large reduction of the capability of the NATO garrison without a changed public policy toward NATO, or without restatement of strategic assumptions, create a circular and superficial debate. Often the critic of current force levels is implicitly assuming modified goals, while the military planner is justifiably defending the appropriate means to achieve *current* goals which have been specifically presented to him by political leadership. A dialogue of the deaf frequently results. Useful discussion of policy obviously requires consideration of both ends and means.

Our seamless web of strategy and structure poses a more basic dilemma under current assumptions. A convincing large conventional-war contingency (NATO) makes the articulation of other required options unnecessary. But if that contingency becomes unconvincing due to changed conditions, then forces for all contingencies may be left without adequate justification. Current debate about the NATO contingency presents precisely this problem.

As a practical matter, it may be politically difficult to maintain active forces if they are not clearly tied to an explicit containment scenario—especially to the defense of NATO. Yet most serious observers realize that forces should be retained for alternative missions—as premiums paid for the "insurance policy"—even if the rationale for this judgment is supported primarily by the history of U.S. requirements for ground power outside of Europe since World War II. We fought the Vietnam War largely with "NATO" forces; the Expeditionary Forces we sent into Lebanon and the Dominican Republic were "NATO" forces. Had we invaded Cuba in 1962, the ground forces used would have been "NATO" forces.

Dependence on NATO cuts far deeper than that. NATO has not only been the principal generator of forces for alternative uses, but it has provided the rationale for a certain desirable redundancy which is built into the institutional structure. Where, for example, would the thousands of combat arms generalists which were available to be used as Vietnam advisors have come from had a European land warfare contingency not been motivating the size and training of the Army?

We believe that we need to have a better way of designing our forces—a way which takes new factors into account and which provides for change if we are to support a flexible, coalition approach to security. The risks and disadvantages of an indefinite continuation of the current rationale are simply too great. The status quo offers an inadequate basis for force design for meeting many likely future contingencies; it leads to increasing divergence between actual resources committed to meet containment contingencies, and those resources "required" based upon containment assumptions which are not explicitly changed. Lastly, continuation of the current rationale could deprive the nation of needed non-NATO contingency forces should European commitment be substantially downgraded.

FORCE DEVELOPMENT FOR COALITION SECURITY

The insurance-policy analogy mentioned in the opening chapter illustrates a very general rationale for the retention of military forces, but at the same time suggests the difficulty in being precise about requirements. How does one go about designing actual forces for the future? The future is unknowable. Each person weighs the resources which should be devoted to hedging against uncertainty. Individuals each consider different degrees of risk to be prudent and acceptable. Underlying these values are widely varying assumptions about what kinds of uncertainties we ought to hedge against anyway.

The preceding chapters assessed the context in which the Army must operate in support of national security policy. Certain conclusions which flow from that assessment can be stated in the form of general guidelines for force development in the emerging period:

(1) Commitment to sustained conventional war (on the model of World War II) should be downgraded as a basis for force development and planning.

(2) Commitment to an "internal defense" counter-insurgency model as a guide should be downgraded as well.

(3) Utility of ground forces must be derived primarily from optimization of active force capabilities with relatively less reliance placed upon employment of reserve forces in a wide range of contingencies.

(4) Greater consideration must be given to potential nuclear weapons employment in the design and employment of active ground forces, especially in the NATO context.

These guidelines illustrate the problem of designing and employing active volunteer forces which have inherently limited capabilities but which must still be effective in a wide range of contingencies in support of policy. The aim of designing forces in accordance with these guidelines is neither to make it easier to enter into a sustained war nor to suggest nuclear weapons as a means of compensating for the limitations of ground power. Rather it is to provide us new choices which support policy at minimum risk and which hedge against both political and military uncertainty. These new options would call for substantial changes in our current approach involving both organization and strategy.

These rather sobering and constrictive conclusions are a necessary precondition to developing those new choices. They can serve to establish some broad parameters within which we should operate. But obviously a more positive basis is needed to provide guidance. Against what contingencies should we hedge by maintaining forces? What capabilities do these "hedges" entail? What type of force would give us these capabilities? How should the force be employed? These are the thorny questions to which the force planner and strategist must address himself.

To begin with we must acknowledge the fact that no specific requirement for particular forces can be proven. We can go no further than being honest, persuasive, and consistent with our assumptions, for we are dealing with probabilities, not certainties. The contingencies are largely "unannounced," unlike the Cold War contingencies, many of which were in effect announced by national policy.

TOWARD GREATER STRATEGIC FLEXIBILITY

The Army force needed for the 1970s in support of coalition security should possess greater strategic flexibility to support a foreign policy which employs selective involvement, rather than extensive static, overseas stationing of U.S. ground forces as "hostages".

Substantial reorientation is required for this. Current forces possess substantial capability but they do not maximize the flexibility required to respond rapidly to a range of non-NATO-type contingencies. This is due largely to our current dependence on either a continuous draft or mobilization to permit deployment of forces. Certainly we cannot responsibly put aside current realities and commitments in pursuit of a desired future policy. Therefore forces for the 1970s must continue to meet existing commitments, in the context of a reshaping of the overall picture. The capabilities required of Army forces therefore must include continued maintenance of the NATO and Korean commitments during a transitional era in which our focus is shifting. Table 4-2 suggests the changing strategic calculation in geographic terms.

The orientation during the period of transition is in flux and subject to management. But the direction is nonetheless clear. The challenge is to build toward a force compatible with the emerging demands, while sustaining adequate current capability.

TABLE 4-2
PROBABILITY OF EMPLOYMENT (in percentages)

	Europe	Middle East	Far East & South America
1950s	70	10	20
		Transition	
1970s	33	33	33

A "READY ARMY" FOR
COALITION SECURITY

What is needed is an Army which is more explicitly designed for, and justified on the basis of, rapid deployment in support of a broad range of contingencies, with reduced reliance upon mobilization. While the current force possesses great capability, much of available resources are devoted to buying deferred power. That is, substantial sums are consumed by purchasing an ability to man, equip, and deploy units which would be mobilized at time of need. To a certain extent this is at the expense of current in-being capability. Active forces are largely dependent upon support elements which would require mobilization before being prepared for deployment or sustained operations. This type of force is necessary not only to cope with the contingencies which appear to be of greater relevance for future employment of U.S. forces, but also in order to provide an acceptable alternative to the current basic rationale for forces, the NATO conflict, which has supported large forces in the past but is now becoming less convincing as the Cold War continues to erode. In other words, a "Ready Army" is needed which is both designed and justified on the basis of strategic flexibility. And it must be built and employed within the parameters developed earlier, which are a product of changing attitudes and conditions. This is essential if we are to have both necessary capability for the years ahead and acceptable justification for it.

Strategic flexibility will require more mobile, tailorable, and self-sufficient active forces which can better respond to a variety of contingencies. While perhaps smaller in total numbers than what we now have, active forces need to be better balanced internally and more capital-intensive in order to provide maximum readiness, flexibility, and combat power in being. An army composed of several rapidly deployable corps-sized forces is a concept worth examining in some detail. One such corps would maintain a presence in Europe. Another might be Asia-oriented, with one element—perhaps a division—maintaining a presence in Asia and the remainder prepared to reinforce it rapidly. A third might serve as an active strategic reserve based in the United States and oriented toward reinforcing a presence abroad or establishing a new one, perhaps in the Middle East. Even if most or all of our forces were to be redeployed eventually to the United States, the basic orientation and organization would remain. Corps of the type suggested should be highly mobile and deployable in brigade-size increments if necessary. Appropriate air and other support elements would need to be similarly packaged. Our Marine Corps divisions would of course complement this capability, although their primary task would be the traditional one of supplementing and extending our seapower. A more detailed portrayal of the characteristics of this force is included in Chapter 9.

How would this general posture differ from current Army force configuration? The qualitative differences would be substantial, and of even greater importance than quantitative ones. A key feature is greater in-being capability for active forces. The basic change in orientation of active forces would be as shown in Table 4-3, eventually corresponding to a new strategic orientation.

A type, or hypothetical, Army which would conform to this concept would resemble the force shown in Figure 4-2. The numbers which are illustrated in this diagram are of

TABLE 4-3

FLEXIBLE RESPONSE VS. COALITION SECURITY:
ARMY DIVISION ORIENTATION

	Flexible Response	Coalition Security
Europe	8 Div.	1 Corps*
Asia	1 Div.	1 Corps
Strategic Reserve	4 Div.	1 Corps

*Corps consist of variable number of divisions, usually from 3 to 5.

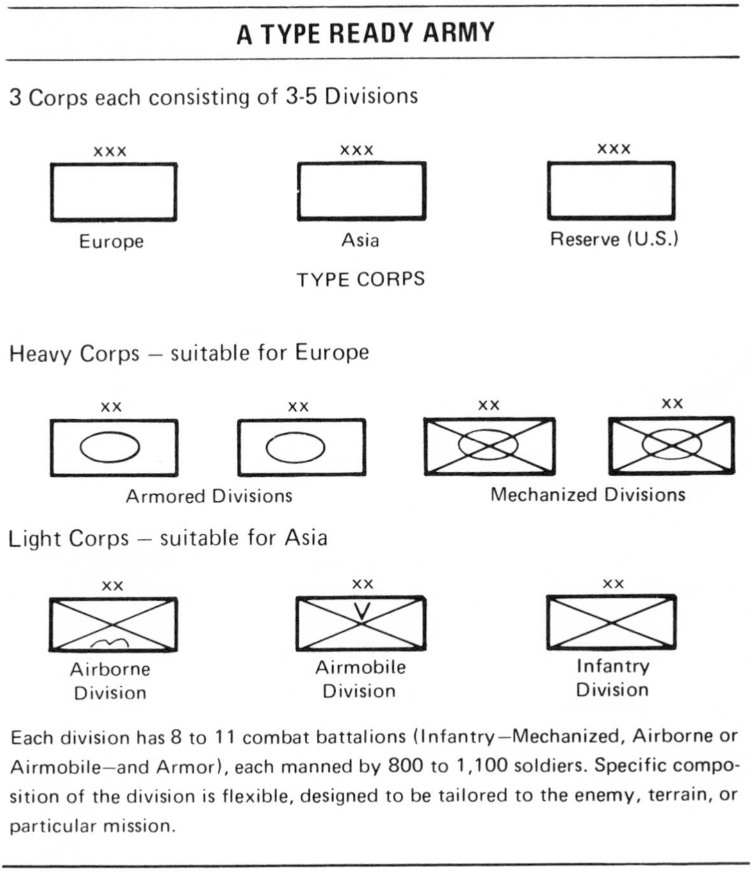
A TYPE READY ARMY
3 Corps each consisting of 3-5 Divisions
XXX
XXX
XXX
Europe
Asia
Reserve (U.S.)
TYPE CORPS
Heavy Corps – suitable for Europe
XX
XX
XX
XX
Armored Divisions
Mechanized Divisions
Light Corps – suitable for Asia
XX
XX
XX
Airborne Division
Airmobile Division
Infantry Division
Each division has 8 to 11 combat battalions (Infantry—Mechanized, Airborne or Airmobile—and Armor), each manned by 800 to 1,100 soldiers. Specific composition of the division is flexible, designed to be tailored to the enemy, terrain, or particular mission.

Figure 4-2.

less significance than the concept of a Ready Army force of three corps designed to provide flexibility and multiple capability. Corps have been chosen because they are the smallest expeditionary force with adequate combat capability and self-contained command, control, and support to constitute a significant U.S. military presence in a variety of environments. The units required for the active Army would be those which are absolutely essential and which could not be mobilized quickly from reserve components.

To move toward such a Ready Army from the current force would call for substantial restructuring over a considerable period. Units excess to the future Ready Army would not be disestablished. They are present to respond to current commitments. However as forces are restructured for coalition security operations the concept of a baseline Ready Army of three contingency corps would serve to define the prudent minimum for configuring the bulk of active forces. It would also entail substantial modifications in the reserve structure. These changes will be dealt with in detail later.

GENERAL EMPLOYMENT CONCEPTS

How would these Army forces be configured and employed? There are two major criteria to be met. The first concerns the adequacy of forces for achieving policy goals. It might be termed policy "sufficiency". To support policy objectives, a deployed force must obviously be sufficient to achieve whatever limited goals for which it is employed. Sufficiency of forces for this must nearly always be based upon a mixture of both political and military judgment, depending upon the goals and circumstances of employment. If the goal is primarily deterrence, as it is in Europe, it is largely political. In that context deterrence involves more than merely a unilateral U.S. military capability. A deployed "deterrent" force contributes to a total allied political-military posture which should be sufficient to raise the price of military adventurism to an unacceptable level for the enemy, to include forcing him to calculate the risk of prompting a nuclear response. Our deployed ground units thus contribute to a conventional option in this environment by having a credible ability to commit the United States in conjunction with allies and by creating a context in which the possession of a nuclear capability is meaningful. Sufficient combat power to meet the criterion of sufficiency is therefore a question largely of political judgment, within broad limits.

It is important to remember, however, that deterrence is not the only purpose for developing a conventional option, and while Europe is clearly vital, it is not the only area in which our interests are affected. It is conceivable that other limited policy goals might require a conventional option provided by ground power. These goals may be such that there is little to distinguish between political and military assessments of what is needed, and thus there is virtual overlap between them. An example might be the employment of a landing force to evacuate threatened American citizens from a foreign city or port.

The characteristics of sufficiency just described are of course basic since it would clearly be pointless to deploy forces inadequate to support the positive objectives of policy. These characteristics of the criterion of sufficiency have quite naturally been the point of departure for structuring forces to be deployed and for developing plans for their employment.

But we should also consider an additional criterion, which might be called "survivability" of deployed forces. This would mean simply that the minimum force we would deploy would have the capability to survive in the face of any conventional attack without substantial reinforcement from the United States.

While such a criterion would have validity under any circumstances, it is of particular importance to any current assessment owing to the changing constraints on military power discussed earlier in conjunction with the continued presence of nuclear weapons. Survivability would insure that we will not be faced with an undesirable choice between nuclear weapons or the loss of a large force in the event that deployed forces become deeply committed and the nation cannot, or chooses not, to substantially reinforce or otherwise enter a sustained war.

This concept of survivability can be explained best in terms of NATO. A generation of peace argues powerfully in support of the wisdom of our political assessments concerning the general sufficiency of the forces there. Deterrence has succeeded. But what has been needed for deterrence? In the complex NATO-Warsaw Pact milieu it is a largely political assessment of allied and enemy resolve, capabilities, and intentions, of estimated future interests of numerous parties, and a wide variety of other factors over and above our own combat capability on the ground in Europe. This is in the nature of things—the world is a complicated place, not neatly compartmentalized into political and military affairs. But nevertheless, there is a core military consideration here. If a conflict were to start in Europe, could our forces sustain themselves without a nuclear escalation if for some reason NATO forces as a whole failed to halt a Warsaw Pact attack? It may very well be that they could. But if through some shift in balance of forces or other circumstances it were to become clear that U.S. forces faced destruction, then in effect the President would have only a Hobson's choice between nuclear escalation and an unsuccessful American Dunkirk should deterrence fail.

History offers some examples which illustrate the kind of choice we want to avoid. Looking to our own experience, the defeat of American forces in the Philippines at the beginning of World War II can be cited. Could our President have survived the disasters of Bataan and Corregidor had they not been preceded by a whole series of unprecedented events, including the fall of France and the attack on Pearl Harbor, which generated an atmosphere of world crisis in which our cause became transformed into virtually a moral crusade? Had nuclear weapons been available to him, would President Roosevelt have employed them against the Japanese overwhelming our forces under Douglas MacArthur? Would he have had any real choice *not* to use them and remain President? While our forces in the Philippines were not sufficient to survive against the conventional power of the enemy, the environment was then non-nuclear. Today it is not.

Another important reason for considering a criterion of survivability is its potential as a meaningful basis for force structuring on military grounds. For example, should future political leaders examine the feasibility of reducing our NATO garrison to a genuine trip-wire force of perhaps one or two divisions, it would be most difficult for military professionals to argue against this within the terms currently employed—those of deterrence. But would such a reduction in forces be prudent? Here survivability should come into focus. It can serve as a means of arguing for a balanced organization of sufficient size and composition to be a credible conventional force. Further, it is a concept which falls clearly within professional military responsibility and competence.

History provides an illustration. When Hitler sent his small token force into the Rhineland in 1936 to remilitarize it in defiance of the Treaty of Versailles and the large French Army, he was taking a political gamble. His generals were right to tell him that it was an unsupportable decision on military grounds alone, for French forces could easily have destroyed the German units. As it turned out, his political judgment was vindicated since the French and the other treaty signatories acquiesced. Furthermore, Hitler was probably willing to lose the entire German force. But his military advisors made the potential costs of the policy clear. Had he erred in his political judgment and the German force been annihilated, perhaps he then would have been seen as an irresponsible, rather than a merely audacious, political leader. The point is that his correct political judgment does not vitiate the correct military judgment of his advisors, nor could it serve as any rational basis for designing a task force.

We may again turn to NATO for illustration. There is a reasonably precise means of estimating what combat capabilities alternative U.S. forces, including our current one, would possess in a combat withdrawal to the west in the face of conventional enemy pressure without substantial reinforcement or allied assistance. The minimum adequate force is probably on the order of several heavy divisions supported by substantial air cover. In fact, the minimum survivable force may be larger than the current four and one-third divisions in Europe. But for deterrence a necessary U.S. contribution to the alliance may be significantly more or less than that. Indeed, our economic and cultural reliance on Europe may even contribute to that purpose. As a practical matter, should deployed forces be reduced below what professional military judgment considers to be a prudent minimum to survive, it would be the responsibility of the military advisor to make this clear to the decision-maker. Obviously there could be alternative options for survival in a given situation. But the differences between these in terms of resource requirements could be measured with a fair amount of accuracy and their implications examined.

To be consistent with these employment concepts, active forces stationed in the United States would require sufficient logistic support on hand for immediate and rapid deployment and sustainability in combat without substantial reinforcement. A goal would be to develop the capability to deploy a full corps with required support elements to an overseas theater without mobilization. Therefore, sufficient direct support elements—those needed for survival in combat—should be retained in the active structure for these forces.

CHARACTERISTICS OF THE
READY ARMY

We believe that active Army force elements require the following characteristics to support coalition security:

Self-sustaining—Sufficient active combat and logistic support capabilities to conduct operations in the theater of operations for a specified period of time without substantial reinforcement;

Sufficient Capability—Sufficient combat power so that major military forces would be necessary to dislodge it;

Survivability—Able to disengage and withdraw from theater of operations without assistance from allies, if necessary; and

Tailored to environment where likely to be employed.

These characteristics would enhance the Army's ability to maintain the following required general capabilities: The Ready Army could deploy to any geographic area. It could establish and maintain military presence in that area. It could conduct ground operations in that area unilaterally or as part of an allied force. It could deny enemy control of that area and it could deploy intact with or without allied assistance. However, it could not conduct sustained large-scale ground operations without mobilization of reserves and activation of a draft.

We believe the Ready Army is adapted to the uncertainties of the international situation in the 1970s, and that it provides the minimum level force possessing the capability to meet military requirements of this decade. It does not depend upon any particular set of international conditions for its justification. It calls for a tolerable level of defense expenditures and manpower resources. Finally it provides a basis for analysis of additional force requirements to meet specific threats or other needs.

SCENARIOS FOR HYPOTHETICAL
EMPLOYMENT

The maintenance of physical military presence on land masses abroad, while feasible and desirable in the transitional near-term as a part of our treaty commitments, may not be a permanent condition. When circumstances no longer permit and require them, our Army ground forces would be withdrawn to the United States. But their role would continue to be that of providing the capability to interpose rapidly presences of the type described above into vital land areas abroad. A key task for military planners therefore would be to develop scenarios for likely general-purpose force employment in key areas in order to determine the strategic mobility and other logistical assets required to support contingency deployments. Any mobilization strategy would have to be designed to support rapid, responsive, and selective employment.

There is a wide range of hypothetical contingencies which will continue to pose potential challenges to the United States and the Army. The range of possible contingencies remains unchanged from the past. But their ordering in terms of priority for planning has undergone adjustment. Furthermore, all do not apply with equal probability to major and minor powers nor are they necessarily related to containment patterns of the past. The range of contingencies suggests a variety of potential military roles:

Deterrence of strategic nuclear war;
General war (non-strategic);
Limited war (possibly with tactical nuclear weapons);
Stability operations;
Diplomatic support;
Peacekeeping;
Conflict prevention;
Resource protection;

Disaster relief;
Foreign military training.

The strategic nuclear war and general contingencies would involve major powers. As suggested earlier, their probability of occurring appears on the decline in an era of coalition security. Their occurrence would risk destruction of the balance-of-power system itself, which is in the interest of no major power. Yet a continued hedge against these remains important and requires contributions from each military service, as shown in Table 4-4.

The third category, limited war, can involve major and minor powers, and the contribution of each service is potentially large, depending on specific conditions and policy objectives in a limited war situation. Much of the earlier discussion concerning employment concepts with regard to Europe illustrates the considerations which should motivate Army planning for this kind of contingency. This form of conflict in some ways constitutes a hazy dividing line or threshold within the spectrum of contingencies. Below this threshold ground forces become of increasing relative significance while the contingencies for their use become increasingly probable. Figure 4-3 illustrates this schematically.

TABLE 4-4

	Strategic Exchange	General War
Army	ABM	Armored/mechanized divisions
		Tactical nuclear weapons
		Control of ground
Air Force	ICBM	Tactical air support
	Bombers	Air lift
		Control of air
Navy	Polaris	Sea lift
	Fighter bombers	Tactical air (limited)
		Marines
		Control of sea

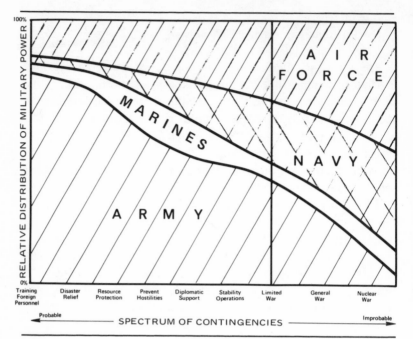

Figure 4-3.

Several hypothetical situations may serve to illustrate potential employment of ground forces and illustrate possible missions for the active Ready Army. Not all involve actual hostilities.

—Assume that North Korea threatens hostile action against South Korea by mobilizing forces. The U.S. could demonstrate a capability and willingness to support South Korea through the following actions:

Army: major elements of the Asia-oriented corps would reinforce the garrison present in South Korea. Armored/mechanized elements would arrive by sea, lighter elements would be air-landed.

Air Force: strategic airlift and tactical air support on call would be provided.

Navy: sea lift, capability to establish beachheads (Marines), security of sea lanes.

A comparable contingency can be envisioned in the Middle East, but with greater visibility given to the potential use of tactical nuclear weapons:

—Assume that Soviet-backed Arab forces are conducting successful operations which threaten the survival of Israel. There is clear and present danger of introduction of nuclear weapons. The U.S. would interpose a conventional/tactical nuclear presence to stabilize the situation.

Army: major elements of a heavy corps (armored and mechanized forces) would be introduced into Israel.

Air Force: provide air cover, tactical air support on call, and a nuclear umbrella.

Navy: provides carrier air support, sea lift, and maintenance of lines of communication.

We may also envision serious threats to vital resources which can be secured only by possession of credible intervention capability:

—Assume severe unrest in the Persian Gulf oil-producing states. Soviet or Chinese-backed radical regimes initiate military action, threatening Western and Japanese sources of oil. The U.S. could intervene to support the independence of Gulf states and to demonstrate capability of protecting resource supplies.

Army: land sufficient forces to protect vital resources, initial elements airlanded from strategic reserve corps.

Air Force: provide airlift, tactical air on call.

Navy: provide sea lift, resupply, protection of sea lanes.

Rapid deployment to support coalition obligations would also require appropriate forces:

—Assume Soviet efforts to further fragment Pakistan by support of separatist movement in western provinces through Afghanistan. In coalition with China (People's Republic), the U.S. would act to prevent dismemberment:

Army: provide materiel, tactical helicopter air lift, technicians, reconnaissance elements to Pakistan; alert deployable ground elements to intervene in event of cross-border hostilities.

Air Force: air lift to Pakistan and China.

Navy: sea lift, supply routes.

These are but a few of the type contingencies for which scenarios would need to be developed to serve as a basis for planning. Many others, especially in the areas of disaster relief and peacekeeping, would also be required. In each of these cases the ground forces visualized should be immediately deployable without mobilization of reserves or degradation of capabilities required by a need to hedge against other (such as NATO) contingencies.

SUMMARY

If the necessary kinds of capabilities are to be translated into reality, efforts must proceed on several major avenues. Among the principal ones are those listed below.

(1) Enhance in-being combat capability and sustainability of active forces to compensate for reduced reliance on mobilization. This will require better use of technology as well as greater emphasis on balanced task forces for employment. Further, it may be necessary to emphasize greater specialization in force and equipment design in order to develop tailored task forces for contingency employment.

(2) Develop appropriate complementary role for reserve components: This will be essential to adjust to the changing likelihood of mobilization and to changing priorities of active force employment.

(3) Enhance the capability of the NATO garrison to operate independently without reinforcement: This is essential to insure

that our largest force currently committed is structured in line with new realities of sufficiency and survivability.

(4) Reshape Army programs in support of allies to provide greater flexibility for coalition security operations and diplomacy.

The policy implications of each of these guidelines are examined in the subsequent chapters of Part II—the Army and NATO, reserve force policies for the future, Army support of coalition diplomacy, and capital intensification of Army forces. We believe that these four areas pose the most difficult challenges to development of a new Ready Army. Finally, we project the resources required to implement these or similar policies in Chapter 9 on the costs of an Army for coalition security. In that chapter the specific assumptions concerning the capabilities desired are discussed.

Chapter 5

THE ARMY AND NATO

Maintenance of a free, prosperous Western Europe is an enduring vital interest of the United States. Its defense is secured by a complex mixture of military, economic, and political/cultural factors. The military component of the defense equation is an amalgam of U.S. and allied strategic and tactical capability—land, sea, and air. Our concern is to improve one element in European defense—the U.S. Army ground force contribution to NATO. Concentration on this relatively narrow aspect of maintenance of U.S. vital interest in Europe does not imply lack of awareness or appreciation of the extraordinarily complex defense equation. Rather, it reflects concentration on one basic Army mission in coalition security with a view toward improvement of the quality of performance.

The ground force commitment to the defense of Western Europe is the dominant generator of requirements for all U.S. Army forces today. As we discussed in the preceding chapter, Europe produces continuing justification for the maintenance of usable, ready ground military power available for national use within and beyond Europe. This ready capability has been an essential national military asset—the necessary capability to hedge against the unforeseen contingency. For

example, we look back today at the professionalism of 7th
Army in the late 1950s and early 1960s which provided the
large cadre of officer and NCO competence that facilitated
the remarkably successful initial unit deployments to Vietnam—a welcome contrast to the readiness of the first support
forces deployed to Korea. Despite debate as to the size,
composition, and disposition—United States or overseas—of
the U.S. contribution to the ground defense of Western
Europe, acceptance of the need for preserving this military
capability is one of the very few givens in current debate
about national security policy. In these days of painful
readjustments and scarce resources, we must be particularly
alert to provide honest readiness to the nation while gaining
full ground-force capability "value" from the continuing
credibility of the NATO defense commitments and their
requirements.

The desirable size, composition, and structure of the
American contribution to ground defense should be influenced strongly by several current factors: Soviet/Warsaw Pact
capabilities; the changing NATO-Allied Command Europe
(ACE) defense environment; U.S. military reinforcement
capabilities, and current Army readiness for tactical nuclear
warfare.

Soviet/Warsaw Pact ground-force capabilities have continued to improve during the past decade, while the Army's
most capable teachers, resources, schooling emphasis, and
research/development have been focused on counter-
insurgency in a jungle environment. Soviet forces may enjoy
temporary qualitative and quantitative superiority, particularly during the present transitional period of our read-
justment to the Europe situation. The balance can be
redressed if we can successfully blend our vast and unique air
vehicle experience of Vietnam with the development of
doctrine and capability suitable for armored warfare in
Europe. Hopefully, we will perceive and capitalize on
innovations, both allied and Soviet, which matured during

our extended efforts in Asia. We should organize, equip, train, and dispose our NATO force so that it will facilitate rapid development of a highly ready mid-intensity oriented army.

The NATO-ACE defense environment has been changing as Western Europe approaches the dilemmas and the rewards of the modern post-industrial state. The effects have been modification of both the physical characteristics of Central Europe and the attitudes of its peoples. The physical transformation has caused a gradual but significant shift in the military geography. Urbanization spreads along the major transportation arteries—the Rhine plain is becoming a continuous urban area. Suburban life style spawns Levitt-type communities near industrial centers. European Community agricultural policy furthers urbanization and changes the pattern of land cultivation. New political and economic organizations modify patterns and techniques of defense decision-making. As a European Community capital, Brussels gains new political and military importance. In sum, there has been a vast range of change in the physical environment since the U.S. contribution to NATO was structured—relocation of the line of communication (LOC) is the most striking example—yet there has been little if any perceptible redisposing of the U.S. force.

There has been an equally significant shift in popular attitudes created by the approach of the post-industrial state. The new affluence and reduced threat perception create a slow, steady erosion of public support for maintenance of conscript military capability. The issue is more fundamental than anti-militarism. It is a question of subordination of individual rights to a larger bureaucratic organization for a cause of questionable necessity. The antipathy of youth to large impersonal organizations may invalidate traditional assumptions concerning the maintenance of capability during an extended period of apparent detente. Simultaneously it may permit the mobilization of youth on an unprecedented scale to defend their village or suburb. Solution of local problems may be a new stimulus to public service by youth. Local police, local militia defense, and local environmental improvement may replace national service as probable areas of commitment of modern youth. As a result of the emphasis on local services, militia forces may be the only form of defense commitment acceptable to many Europeans. Our contribution to NATO ground defense should be responsive to the potential of this distinctly new post-industrial environment which may necessitate increased reliance on militia forces rather than on traditional national conscription armies.

The structure of our NATO ground defense establishment must also be influenced by our wartime ability to reinforce Europe. The combination of a decreasing U.S. Merchant Marine fleet, increasing Soviet sea and undersea naval capability, and Soviet air and missile ability to interdict air reinforcement serves to question our ability to increase the contribution to NATO defense once hostilities commence. There has been a major change in the capabilities and vulnerabilities of the strategic lines of communication since the current NATO ground force was structured and equipped. This change would seem to provide a valid, consistent military rationale for insisting that a balanced war-fighting force must be on the ground before hostilities commence in order to provide a real alternative to the early use of nuclear weapons and to ensure that there is a "survivable" force if deterrence and alliance both fail.

A fourth major determinant of the ability of our NATO force should be the level of preparedness for the employment of tactical nuclear weapons. As frequently measured by the number of tactical nuclear weapons and delivery units maintained in Europe, there is a popular expectation that our NATO forces are well prepared for conflict on the nuclear battlefield. This may be a questionable expectation. Necessary preoccupation with the problems of counter-insurgency for an extended period has weakened the already limited assimilation and readiness of the Army to engage in tactical nuclear conflict. For example, significant doctrinal and capability gaps in individual and collective protection or decontamination for more than a brief period and unrealistic service school instruction undercut the confidence and genuine capability required at unit level if the use of tactical nuclear weapons is to be a rational albeit desperate policy. To the limited extent that there are fads in expectations of war, the fad of the fifties was tactical nuclear warfare; the fad of the sixties was counter-insurgency. The truth, and genuine capability in defending Europe, lies well between.

NEW DIRECTIONS

Based upon the objectives of the ground commitment to NATO and the new factors acting, we should consider a new direction for the U.S. Army contribution to NATO defense. This alternative is raised in full realization of the complexity of European defense issues. We acknowledge that discussion of minimum land-force requirements based upon survivability assumptions (particularly lack of allied support) and associated redisposing might have a destabilizing effect on maintenance of deterrence. We can ill afford to jar gratuitously a complex psychological framework which has been the keystone of successful defense of Western Europe. However, we are equally aware that current discussions (particularly negotiations about Mutual Balanced Force Reduction) raise fundamental defense issues. Major restructuring of European defense may permit if not require consideration of heretofore closed issues. For example, a restructuring of the U.S. ground force contribution could be a useful catalyst stimulating the development of a Western European defense organization with credible independent nuclear means. This could be the military backbone for superpower status in the European Community.

First, U.S. force requirements for NATO should be reevaluated to ensure that U.S. Army Europe possesses, as a minimum, a wholly ready, balanced corps capable of conducting a conventional delay to one or more embarkation sites with little warning and without reliance on allied military forces in the face of conventional Warsaw Pact attack. All essential ground line of communications (LOC) forces would be maintained in Europe continuously. The "rock bottom" force requirement would be based upon the bare minimum military capability for survival. It would in all probability be comparable to or larger than current U.S. forces stationed in Germany. The total actual force necessary for defense on the ground would probably be larger. Additional U.S. forces would undoubtedly be required to accomplish NATO's goals of forward ground defense and flexible response on an allied basis. These additional forces could be maintained either on the continent or preferably in the United States as a second three-to-five division "Europe-reinforcing" corps prepared for rapid delivery prior to hostilities. (For discussion of reinforcement alternatives see Table 9-1 in Chapter 9.)

Second, the USAREUR corps (three to five divisions, with exact number to be determined by MBFR outcome) would be organized, trained, and equipped to permit calculated employment of tactical nuclear weapons. Representative necessary measures include increased Chemical Biological Radiological (CBR) decontamination and survey capability; extended training in a simulated radioactive environment (two to four days requiring protective clothing); increased off-road mobility for support units; mobile fuel, ammunition, and river crossing prestocks; and reinstitution of Nuclear Weapons Employment training for the majority of combat arms officers.

A significant restructuring of the U.S. force would

probably be required to ensure a successful outcome in a tactical nuclear battlefield. Some type of overwatching tactical nuclear command possessing superior target acquisition, separate communications, and highly flexible mobile fire power would be necessary. This may be a uniquely valuable use of the new capabilities now being tested. In any event, there must be genuine capability to employ tactical nuclear weapons in retaliation as a considered military course of action.

Third, USAREUR forces would be redisposed to occupy a central reserve position astride the most critical avenues of Soviet attack. Redisposing could occur as one element in continent-wide arms control measures or to complement the development of supplemental European militia forces responsible for immediate local defense. We could envisage a well-balanced heavy armor corps disposed on the North German plain in the general vicinity of the borders with Benelux. This force would be located to back up German militia forces heavily armed with the TOW or Dragon anti-tank weapons and reinforced with allied reconnaissance elements. (Tube launched, Optically tracked, Wire guided [TOW] is a recently developed heavy anti-tank weapon for the infantry. When matched with the Cobra attack helicopter for anti-tank capability, it is known as the Cobra-TOW.) In effect, evolution of anti-tank weapons has created the potential of genuine anti-armor capability maintainable by militia forces.

Placement of the U.S. force in a critical reserve location would provide several advantages. It would enhance deterrence by insuring that any decisive Soviet attack would meet U.S. ground forces while placing militia or European forces between U.S. forces and border provocations that could arise from unrest in Eastern Europe. Further, it should put U.S. ground forces astride the most direct line of communication and thereby enhance "survivability".

It is interesting to note that in effect we have repositioned our forces in Korea along lines similar to those suggested here for NATO. Combat units remaining have been placed in a position astride the approach to Seoul.

A crucial aspect of repositioning would be that if it were to be accomplished prior to M day, it could compel the return of some or all military dependents to the United States. It does not seem likely that a major family-housing building program would be feasible for all dependents in new development areas. Nor is it necessarily desirable to maintain military dependents in "little Americas". The Army can ill afford the popular image of dispositioning around aging Kasernes whose strategic location in NATO-ACE has always been doubtful. U.S. Army Europe must be far more combat-ready in reality and in image. Prior to the drawdown for Vietnam and associated problems, USAREUR could afford the burdens of maintaining adequate family infrastructure and guarding a secondary axis of attack. We may no longer be able to afford these practices.

Return of some dependents to the United States would precipitate two associated, critically important, self-reinforcing policies: the acceptance of responsibility for the total environment of those dependents in CONUS, and dramatic improvement in training of deployed units. The Army cannot renege on its obligations as a "married Army", that is, the promise of providing a satisfactory family life for its men. Should separated tours become commonplace, the Army must accept increased responsibility for the life style of dependents. For example, some form of unit rotation to Germany for periods of six months to one year would be necessary for those units which would be stationed in Germany without dependents. Family housing and associated facilities would have to be provided for dependents of all members of the unit at a "home" CONUS post. The unit commander would have to accept increased responsibility for the maintenance of an appropriate life style for his unit's dependents—if necessary, to the extent of unit representation remaining in CONUS to assist dependents during deployments. The deployment schedule would depend on size of the sustaining base. (An appropriate guideline could be that the period of deployment should not exceed one-third of a soldier's period of service with the unit.) It might be possible and feasible to provide unit leave to families in CONUS during the deployment.

Troops deployed to Europe would maintain an intensive training program to ensure maintenance of readiness commensurate with the capability of our complex equipment and to reduce normal idle time and disciplinary problems in a foreign environment. All units deployed to Europe would have to be located and funded so that at least half of the time overseas would be spent in the conduct of field training and maneuvers. If adequate training facilities were not available in Europe, units could be rotated to training sites in CONUS. Our most precious and valuable combat asset—the well-trained, disciplined soldier—should be moved by unit to the location most suitable for demanding combat preparation. The economics of air lift provided by such equipment as the C5A should make it sensible to move personnel to training equipment prepositioned in the best available training areas worldwide.

We have discussed only one alternative for our current Army contribution to NATO defense. We acknowledge that this could entail a bitter, perhaps unacceptable element—the return of many dependents to the United States. Many of our most capable officers and NCOs have had multiple unaccompanied tours in Vietnam. We are equally certain, however, that the Army can and must give better return for the national resources devoted to the ground defense of Europe. Redisposing the force appears to us to be a critical and necessary element of improvement.

Chapter 6

RESERVE FORCE POLICIES FOR THE FUTURE

The future of the Reserve Components in an environment of coalition security is one of the most perplexing problems facing the Army today. General unease as to the role of reserves has prevailed since the beginning of the nuclear age with its accompanying emphasis on forces-in-being in lieu of maintenance of a massive mobilization base. Nominally ready reserve forces and reliance on allies have been the relief valves which permitted professional acquiescence to sizeable reductions in the size or readiness of the ground force-in-being in the face of a large and growing Soviet military capability. Provided one did not look too closely at reserve readiness (personnel, training, or equipment), "One Army"—Active Army, National Guard, and Army Reserve—was a necessary, comforting concept. Further, lack of improvement was not strictly an Army problem. State and local politics severely circumscribed the best intentioned programs for improvement.

It seems doubtful that this situation can persist. Without the inducement of the draft, young men may not "vote" to preserve the myth of mobilization capability. We must be prepared to accept new concepts and methods for mobilization expansion. The new concepts should be based on reassessment of the objectives of reserve forces and acknowl-edgment of current realities which will influence any proposals.

Objectives for maintenance of reserve forces are short and simple. First, as a major global power pursuing coalition security policies the United States must maintain a potential to engage in major land conflicts world-wide. The adequacy of employment of other instruments of policy will determine the extent of use or non-use of military forces to achieve national objectives. Certainly as the world approaches multi-polar status—U.S., USSR, Europe, Japan, and China—skillful use of diplomatic or economic leverage should enable achievement of national objectives with less frequent use of military force. This may be a characteristic of coalition security. However, our leverage as a global power is enhanced by the possession of credible military capability at all levels of conflict. Our nation seems to have neither the inclination nor the resources to afford in-being military forces suitable for extended conventional conflict on a major land mass. Therefore, portrayal of ability to engage in such conflict must rest with a credible land force mobilization ability—the reserves. To be credible, the capability must be truly capable of expansion and it must be supported as necessary and proper by the American people.

The second objective is derived from the preceding: that is, the necessity for popular support. In these days of hyper-active concern about conflicting national demands, the reserves must perform socially useful missions to justify the continuing allocation of resources. Waiting for the unforeseen global military contingency may not appear to be sufficiently productive use of resources for many Americans. Continuing national support may require more productive contributions to resolution of other national problems during the interim between military crises. The reserves must be dual-capable in a new sense.

Five current realities influence new conceptual approaches

to reserve readiness; these are current policy, present public attitudes, the reserve "requirements" problem, decreasing comparability between skills of the citizen-soldier and those required by the active Army, and broader public expectations of reserve responsibilities.

Present policy is to improve dramatically the readiness of reserve components by means of better, more intensive training both alone and in association with active Army units. As selected units are provided the most modern equipment, it is planned to use these reserve units as "round-out" forces to fill active army divisions. There is a wide range of excellent, innovative programs being tested which would provide, in concept, rapid transfusions of reserve units to reduced-strength active Army divisions. It remains to be determined whether levels of enhanced reserve readiness are possible so that deployment of the genuinely ready unit would not be delayed. It would seem difficult for a round-out "part-time" unit to achieve continuing levels of readiness comparable to those maintained by manned, equipped, and trained regular forces. If, on the other hand, there are real differences in capability, the responsiveness of the entire active division, which consists at least partially of round-out units, would be reduced to the least common denominator of the less-ready reserve unit. In either case, there is real and continuing danger that "round out" will tend to conceal reductions in active force readiness. On the other hand, future events will determine whether improved reserve readiness is actually feasible in a volunteer non-draft-induced reserve establishment. The incentives and characteristics of present service in the reserves may make a volunteer reserve establishment extraordinarily difficult to maintain.

The success of future recruiting will be influenced decisively by current public attitudes. Unfortunately, in far too many public quarters the present image of reserve components is poor. One popular stereotype portrays the Army reserves as low-strength, poorly trained draft dodgers primarily used today as instruments for maintaining local order. Elements of the stereotype may be all too true. The system of draft deferments focused the wrong kind of attention on the reserve forces. Further, the Army is not the sole master of National Guard training or stationing. Jealous of their prerogatives, state administrations maintain close review of Guard personnel and training. Professional Army standards of readiness and training must be adjusted to meet the concerns and often unique perspectives of state governments. Lastly, the reserve components have been placed in the midst of social turmoil as the enforcers of aggressive measures to regain domestic order. It may be difficult to attract sufficient numbers of young Americans to part-time, semi-civilian service in organizations whose basic image has become, in the eyes of many, the use of force domestically.

Nor is it certain exactly what the military requirements for reserve forces are or should be. Most forces appear to be structured for the European war contingency; yet support of coalition security may require a far broader range of military capabilities than current policies provide, even in the case of Europe. For example, there may not be sufficient consideration of the total defense picture which might exist in the event of major Soviet attack into Western Europe, specifically, the actual ability to maintain the security of the sea and air lines of communications between the U.S. and Europe. Reserve units would be required to reinforce overseac forces very rapidly before the LOC could be cut or became unreliable. Yet capability for rapid overseas deployment in several weeks is an extraordinarily taxing requirement. If the very demanding immediate deployment requirement could not be met, it might be months before the LOC was open and shipping was available to move reserves to Europe or some other location.

We may, in fact, be paying the worst price—a level of enhanced readiness in which the reserves are insufficiently ready to rapidly fill out active army units reinforcing Europe, but in which the reserves are more ready to deploy than the ship and aircraft capability to move these troops in case of full mobilization for major war. Further, there is no indication that the reserve organizations programmed for employment in the defense of Europe are amenable to rapid restructuring to meet the various types of conflict which may, in fact, evolve. By the time reserve forces arrived in Europe, the war could be in the Allied defense, tactical nuclear, or conventional delay phases. Troop unit requirements would vary enormously. Any reserve force concept should possess flexibility commensurate with such a range of possible requirements.

Further, the flexibility should provide potential readiness for a broad range of contingencies that could arise not only in Europe but also in support of coalition security operations elsewhere. Most of the contingencies such as peacekeeping operations would be met with the active establishment, but reserves are, by definition, the necessary hedge against unforeseen eventualities requiring major ground forces. Due to the shifting patterns of military relationships characteristic of coalition security, it is virtually impossible to predict the climate, military geography, or specific military threat against which reserves would be mobilized. The all-purpose—all-weather, all-terrain, all-enemy—characteristics of current reserve forces provide a reasonably effective but expensive response against any conceivable situation. We doubt that the Army can continue to maintain such a high-cost answer to the flexibility requirement.

One alternative would be to design reserve forces so that they provide for rapid training and structuring to respond to any particular requirement as it actually develops.

The fourth reality is a growing dissimilarity between the skills of the average combat soldier and the average American. The heritage of the reserves is the citizen-soldier portrayed by the Minuteman—the sturdy yeoman who threw down his hoe and picked up the rifle in time of need. Not only are there fewer sturdy yeomen as we have become increasingly a white-collar, service-oriented economy, but also the Army demands more complex skills even for the decreasing percentage of men who hold combat jobs. The cost and complexity of equipment in the tank company, artillery battery, and even the infantry company has increased drastically since World War II. There is a prima facie case for substantial modification of the length and intensity of reserve training to accommodate new techniques and equipment. For sufficient and understandable reasons, no major changes have been undertaken. Therefore, it may be necessary to examine new reserve force concepts which are more suited to the skills and needs of today's Americans.

The last reality is broadening public expectation of reserve responsibilities. It seems certain that emerging trends of increased public service activity at the local level will influence reserve force missions and responsibilities. The concept of revenue-sharing is based upon decentralization of authority and public service from the federal level to local authority. Also, increased levels of public affluence have stimulated greater expectations of the standards and quality of public service. The reserve components constitute a valuable, needed public resource with many capable and well-motivated leadership/management-trained personnel. The National Guard and Army Reserve are responsive organizations composed of dedicated public servants who could be available for state or local use in resolution of crucial local problems.

In their present form, reserves are a useful and welcome tie between the Army and the local community but they may be expensive contributors to defense readiness. Modification of the roles and responsibilities of military reserves could provide a more productive social payoff for the national dollar.

NEW FUNCTIONS

In the light of the objectives of reserve forces and in recognition of understandable state and local concern about reserve forces, three alternatives to current policy should be pursued:

(1) The National Guard could be reorganized to become a federally supported State Militia trained, manned, and equipped primarily to conduct emergency relief operations, to maintain domestic order as required, and lastly, to manage state or local efforts to improve the lot of individual citizens. The Militia could undertake a broad range of socially productive tasks perhaps in affiliation with state colleges and universities—tasks such as summer camps to teach basic reading and writing skills to less fortunate youth while developing them physically in an outdoor environment. The Militia, again under state control, could join with union locals to provide vocational training to minority groups or it could provide trained public servants willing to advise local communities in such areas as public health and public transport.

In effect, the present National Guard would be decentralized to provide to each state a federally supported, organized, competently administered public service corps suitable for management of social-welfare-type projects in conjunction with other state or local agencies. Such activities would make the organization, management skills and expertise of the citizen-soldier Guardsman available for the resolution of pressing domestic problems. Funding support would remain from the federal level; however, there would be no direct operational relationship between the active Army and State Militia.

Each Militia would probably have to accept additional responsibilities in time of war. There would be no federalization. However, in addition to the normal state responsibilities, its members could accept crucial defense and installation security missions. In addition, they would be expected to provide leaders (cadre) for lateral transfer into the Army to assist in rapid expansion in the event of mobilization. In return for cadre access to the Militia in time of conflict, the active Army could provide leadership and combat-service support training related to social welfare tasks to selected members of the Militia, as requested by the states.

(2) The Army Reserve would be restructured to provide a highly responsive mobilization training base. The Reserve would consist primarily of training units recruited, organized, trained, and equipped to provide highly sophisticated, imaginative individual and unit training progressing from draftee to deployable combat or support division-sized unit in ten to twelve weeks. The challenge is to capitalize on revolutionary improvements in education and training techniques (such as improved classification, computer-assisted instruction, and advanced simulation techniques) to rapidly convert draftees into units trained and equipped for the specific environment and enemy at the time of conflict.

Acceleration of troop training such as is proposed here should be wholly feasible. We know the core abilities required for each soldier to perform successfully in combat; however, we have not applied the instructional advances made in recent decades. For example, knowing the skills required within a successful infantry platoon, we should be able to create in time of peace alternative simulation environments such as airmobile infantry/insurgency/jungle or mechanized infantry/mid-intensity/temperate zone or mechanized infantry/mid-intensity/desert. In time of war requiring reinstitution of the draft, and knowing the location and nature of the conflict, draftees would be prepared primarily for that conflict. Draftees could learn such basic knowledge as use of weapons, patrolling, and first aid as members of platoons in a simulation environment. We should be able to prepare them for deployment at least as platoons in six to eight weeks and as brigades or divisions in several months.

Similar but less ambitious techniques have been used to develop rapidly squad leaders for Vietnam. The use of such multi-task training systems should be extended; we should be able to make mass military training much more efficient and more capital-intensive. Further, we should develop the techniques and skills as we train the active forces in peacetime.

Cadre for the rapidly created units could be provided from the active force, skilled trained leaders maintained in reserve status in skeleton combat units, the Militia of the states, and accelerated NCO training for particularly capable draftees. Critical personnel with complex support skills could be held in continuing reserve units with specialized financial or self-improvement educational incentives.

Our thesis is simple. We believe that the United States has the technology and the know-how required to make a breakthrough in military training comparable to advances made in other areas of endeavor such as space travel or agriculture. We see the effects of technological change beginning to appear in dramatic improvements in training for active forces—such innovations as the learning-center teaching Training Extension Courses (TEC) at the company level, or the application of laser technology to teaching man-versus-man or tank-versus-tank combat. We see the new self-paced, peer-oriented basic training introduced at Fort Ord. We see the sophisticated helicopter command and control simulations at Fort Benning which could train unit staffs and we see sophisticated audio-visual simulations for teaching leadership. In sum, we see much today which could be tied together and expanded to provide a new dimension in military training. We believe that it should be tested. We know that the Army Reserve could play a unique and essential role in its development and exploitation.

(3) Reserve force policies such as we have outlined would permit basic changes to be made in Army equipment procurement policies. Rather than purchase expensive sets of

equipment for reserve units to be used in the event of some future mobilization, a warm production base would be maintained. Emphasis would be on research and development of new systems with actual production only for the active army and for training purposes in the event of mobilization. It may be necessary, of course, to produce mobilization reserves for unusually long lead-time items such as helicopters and tanks. To complement this change, it may be possible to develop alternative tables of organization and equipment for the several "most likely" contingency operations. As mentioned in an earlier chapter, the Cobra-TOW may be a perfectly adequate tank killer everywhere but Europe, where a sophisticated attack helicopter would be required. Tailoring our war reserve requirements to similar analysis of possible contingencies could further influence procurement policies.

The purpose here is not to propose specific policy revisions. It is merely to suggest that once the reserve equation is broken, there is a substantial reorientation of funds which could be made. Those changes which permit significant reduction of current Army acquisition levels should generate funds required to improve dramatically the training, life style, and job satisfaction of the active forces. We portray a possible range of such changes in Chapter 9.

While these proposals may seem drastic, they reflect an implicit faith that experience, knowledge, and technology should permit the Army to make a major departure from mobilization and training practices over fifty years old. Further, they reflect the certain knowledge that the Army can no longer afford the luxury of sizeable prestocks of increasingly expensive equipment to hedge against a "worst case" contingency.

We believe that obvious necessity for substantive change in current reserve forces policies and practices will mitigate heretofore dominant state and local political interests. The range of feasible change has already broadened during the last several years as revenue-sharing, reapportionment, environmental control, and post-Vietnam skepticism about defense practices impinge upon local political givens. But these are forces beyond the Army's ken. Our task is to present alternatives which provide both the capability and the flexibility necessary to meet the requirements of coalition security.

Chapter 7

ARMY SUPPORT OF COALITION DIPLOMACY

In the opening chapter it was suggested that our approach to foreign nations be adjusted to correspond to changing international conditions. Instead of viewing others simply as either allies or enemies, we should adopt a more realistic and pragmatic point of view. We might consider other nations divided roughly into two groups. One is composed of nations with sufficient power to make them potential competitors. The other consists of lesser powers with whom, for a variety of reasons, favorable relationships are desirable. In the first group we would include the Soviet Union, the People's Republic of China, Japan, and the nations of the European Common Market taken as an entity. These nations, or groups of nations, have the potential to alter the distribution of power through adjustments in their foreign policies, or through domestic policies affecting their military strength. The decision taken by the Chinese leadership, for example, to move toward more friendly relations with the United States has already had the effect of causing the Soviet Union and others to reassess their strategic positions.

A number of lesser powers are important to the United States for other diverse reasons. South Korea and Taiwan have special relationships with the United States because of long-standing treaty arrangements and historical ties. Other states such as Saudi Arabia and Algeria possess resources which are vital to the continued industrial vitality of the United States over the longer term. Many states have unique features. Turkey, for example, in addition to historical ties to the United States also possesses geopolitical significance by virtue of its location in relation to routes of entry into the Mediterranean for Soviet shipping. Israel not only occupies a vital location but also has strong emotional and historical ties to the United States.

The essential point is that many different patterns of relationships are required with regard to foreign powers which a Cold War containment approach cannot accommodate. The Army must be in a position to support these various patterns. Since it obviously is not in a foreign policy-making role, its contribution must lie in facilitating the establishment and maintenance of the kinds of flexible relationships necessary for coalition security.

With regard to advanced powers, the guiding principle behind our dealings must be that responsive alterations in arrangements are feasible. This is essential if we are to have the ability to enter into coalitions with others. Our recent diplomacy with regard to China, for example, had to overcome a complex and rigid set of arrangements developed over the years which assumed permanent hostility—perhaps justified at the time established, but which nevertheless made movement difficult. We would be unwise at this point to develop a whole range of binding arrangements with China. It could well be that at some future point our interests will diverge, perhaps with regard to Japan. To the extent possible, Army programs must be consistent with this philosophy of flexibility. In more purely military terms, the relevant contingencies for which planning is appropriate with regard to large powers are those at the upper end of the spectrum of possible roles shown in Chapter 4, that is, strategic nuclear war, general war, and limited war.

Dealings with lesser powers require specifically tailored approaches and correspondingly appropriate Army programs. The range of variation places a large burden on U.S. diplomacy and the military. If anything, realistic and proper programs with regard to lesser powers require a greater degree of sophistication and specialization because many situations and relationships are unique. It is likely that the dealings with lesser powers may actually include the overt use of force by one party or another more than would similar dealings among greater powers. This is because the constraints are often less restrictive, and the potential for large-scale conflict which could alter the global system is either impossible or remote. Referring again to the range of contingencies in Chapter 4, those of lesser magnitude than limited war seem of greatest relevance for guiding Army programs, although limited war is certainly a possibility, as both the Korean and Vietnam Wars amply demonstrate.

NEW DIRECTIONS–ADVANCED POWERS

Our strategic concepts for the employment of ground power and military-assistance programs must be mutually reinforcing. The ability to establish rapidly a credible American presence—without a major mobilization—is a key means by which we could bolster a coalition without inadvertent long-term prior commitment. This will require, however, a change in much of our military training and education toward greater emphasis on independent-type operations. To preserve options—to avoid becoming hostages to partners—requires a capacity to deploy and shift forces quickly. The posture of forces deployed in support of coalitions should be flexible. In Europe, for example, the disposition of our forces does not lend itself readily to making adjustments should we choose to do so as conditions change. We may find it increasingly inconvenient to support inflexibly disposed forces and bases which can become hostages to opposing interests.

Of course, there is inevitably a price to be paid in exchange for the advantages of a coalition. Some independence of movement must be given up. But this should be kept as limited as possible. An historical case which draws the issue clearly is that of Gen. John J. Pershing's rejection of French demands that American soldiers be assigned individually to French units. The United States Army fought as an army, and the United States could therefore take independent diplomatic actions.

We must also accept the fact that long-term cooperative ventures such as cooperative weapons development arrangements at our expense may run counter to the need to keep our options open. Attempts to develop a new tank jointly with the Federal Republic of Germany illustrates the kinds of complexities which major long-term projects can create. Cooperation should not extend to the point that a primary weapons system is subject to the decision of another, even friendly, nation. The unhappy experience of the British resulting from their decision to rely upon the stand-off Skybolt missile is a case in point. British strategic capabilities were hostage to U.S. Department of Defense weapons systems development decisions.

Despite our primary concern about the limits of interdependence, there is another side of the coin. Certain basic requirements must be fulfilled if close military cooperation is to be possible with allies on short notice. If our forces are to be employable in conjunction with allied forces, a certain basic logistical and communications infrastructure must be present and operating procedures of all forces must be mutually understood. Assistance programs must therefore concentrate on sharing technical managerial knowledge, and on developing means by which common operating procedures can be developed and practiced.

A principal avenue toward improving our ability to employ American power abroad must be officer education. We should place greater emphasis on education of our officer corps to foreign military capabilities and procedures. Specifically, we should reduce the number of officers pursuing higher degrees in the general area of international affairs and institute more comprehensive courses of study on international military developments (comparative defense policy), in the neglected area of strategic military contingency planning, and in world economic geography. Service school curricula should also reflect this emphasis. In general, we must begin to train and educate more military planners better prepared for a coalition security environment.

In summary, in order to support coalition security with regard to major powers, the Army should:

—configure forces for rapid deployment without mobilization;

—enhance capability for independent operations;

—where possible, re-dispose forward deployed force to develop greater flexibility;

—limit involvement in cooperative weapons development ventures with foreign nations;

—shape assistance programs toward sharing procedures and developing compatible support structures;

—de-emphasize international relations schooling for officers in favor of military planning and training in subjects such as economic geography.

NEW DIRECTIONS—LESSER POWERS

With regard to the second group of nations—the lesser powers—a different set of problems exists. The larger, more advanced powers have already achieved a high level of technical self-sufficiency and our task is to devise means of working with them in the international arena. But for smaller powers wide distinctions exist both in terms of technical development and goals.

For those closely dependent upon us, especially those which have relied heavily upon us in the past, the challenge is to assist them in reaching a level of capability which is both appropriate to their situations and which does not require substantial U.S. support over the long term. This means that we—and these recipients of our military assistance—should recognize that while a direct role for U.S. forces is inadvisable in a wide range of conventional situations, it is equally inappropriate for many allied nations to attempt to build forces which will be beyond their own capability to sustain.

In this regard, we must be careful not to force foreign military forces into our own mold, either by design or inadvertance. We should exploit and capitalize upon the unique contributions which each partner can make. The Army has much to offer in the way of technical training, organizational concepts, and the techniques essential to modern management. But the guiding philosophy must be that our purpose has two essential objectives. First, we should help the allied force to develop to its full indigenous potential. Second, as is the case with the larger powers, we should work to perfect the interface between our forces and theirs. Such an interface would facilitate combined efforts if our direct assistance ever becomes necessary.

On the first point, to take a simple case, we should not encourage most of our Asian allies to attempt to maintain modern armored or helicopter forces. These would require interminable dependence upon us for support and assistance —to the ultimate detriment of both parties. Rather, we should in most cases assist in such things as tactical communications, light weapons, and small unit training techniques which have a large pay-off in terms of building an adequate ground force but which do not require a heavy investment of funds or large maintenance efforts. (While desirable, this may not always be possible. If the potential or actual enemies of allies are being given advanced weaponry, then we may have no choice but to do likewise. But as a general rule we should work toward more modest goals.) In extension of these efforts we should encourage exchange of instructors at all levels of our service schools with instructors at allied schools.

On the second point, we should concentrate on those areas where coordination of a high degree will be needed to work together effectively. An example here would be the development of common training for personnel necessary for directing artillery fire and air strikes. This idea of "complementarity" should apply to the area of equipment also. Both parties should be capable of maintaining common items such as rifles, trucks, and small unit radios. Where practical, these items should be standard to both forces. This would assist in working together smoothly and using common facilities in the event of a combined effort. Once this complementarity of procedures and equipment has been achieved, sophisticated support could be provided by more militarily advanced U.S. allies. For example, South Vietnam might be provided capital-intensive assistance by more advanced Asian powers rather than by the U.S.

The ability to provide this type of capability is one which requires well-trained personnel with knowledge both of the military needs and capabilities of selected potential allies, and of our own operational procedures. In view of our changing assessment of how we should assist "third world" nations —one which de-emphasizes direct intervention in insurgency situations in favor of indirect help—we might well consider redefining the mission of the Military Assistance Center at Fort Bragg. Emphasis could be placed there upon training officers with knowledge and skills to facilitate complementarity rather than training in internal defense and development. This would be a meaningful and much needed new mission for a number of highly motivated and able Special Forces personnel trained for purposes which are now being downgraded after Vietnam.

Another set of considerations applies also. It was mentioned earlier that a broad range of contingencies involving the employment of ground forces have their highest probability of occurrence with the lesser powers. These contingencies range from peacekeeping operations to disaster relief and foreign military training. Feasible scenarios of U.S. action require detailed planning and expert knowledge of local conditions. For many contingencies, such as disaster relief, joint scenarios are necessary for effective use of American resources. This means that a key challenge to the Army is to develop the necessary planning capability to make our dealings with the lesser powers effective. This function could well be combined with the new training function suggested above for the Military Assistance Center.

In summary, the means by which the Army should seek to enhance its ability to support dealings with lesser foreign nations is by a reshaping of the activities at the Military Assistance Center along the following lines:

—develop training techniques and train cadres, for instructing foreign personnel in U.S. procedures and equipment;

—develop, jointly with the foreign nation where appropriate, contingency plans for the use of Army resources employed in coordination with other services;

—provide specialized training in local conditions of specific nations where Army expertise might be required.

Chapter 8

CAPITAL INTENSIFICATION OF ARMY FORCES

"Capital-intensive" can be interpreted to mean many different things. In general it is a relativistic concept, used as contrasting with "labor-intensive"—that is, using more capital (equipment and machinery) and less labor. But in connection with the design of our ground forces it has a more explicit meaning derived from both quantitative and qualitative factors: a volunteer Army needs to be both smaller and capable of greater combat capability per man and per basic tactical unit. Both smaller *and* better are not necessarily compatible objectives. The danger is that we could end up simply smaller, and not better. It is not merely a question of getting more potent and "sophisticated" equipment into the hands of a few number of men, but of finding the right qualitative/quantitative size of (1) enough *men* who are good enough to use equipment which will exercise their effectiveness, and (2) *equipment* which is adequate for this, but neither too expensive nor too complicated. This means that we can become trapped in an ascending spiral of quality requirements—better equipment requires better men and this will mean fewer men and so we will need better equipment, and so on. But this may be primarily a theoretical dilemma. Most men are going to be average, and their numbers are not going to be determined by scientific means. Politics, and where we have been rather than where we think we ought to go, will play large roles.

As a practical matter, the general thrust of efforts toward greater capital intensification in the remarks that follow will be toward attempting to make better use of the average soldier through better utilization of his own skills, and better use of current technology. This is made necessary because both manpower and dollars are likely to become increasingly scarce.

FACTORS

Manpower and Dollars

There are several related factors which dictate greater capital intensification of our forces in the future. The first is the prospect of greater or even total reliance upon volunteers. The increased manpower costs associated with this require both reduced reliance upon numbers of men and more efficient use of our personnel. A generation or more of the draft has led to an ingrained attitude that basic military manpower is virtually a free good. In a society in which the costs of services has led to the almost total extinction of such species as housemaids, gardeners, and unskilled workers, the Army has continued to operate in an assumed environment of cheap labor. Within the world's most advanced industrial society, in which labor has become the principal cost factor in manufactured goods, the Army has found it not unprofitable to use young able-bodied men as substitutes for machines across a range of activities from leaf raking and police detail to combat operations. This is not due exclusively or even primarily to any peculiar military perspective. Rather it is due to long continuation of a national policy which has in effect subsidized reliance on low-cost manpower by means of the draft. Pay policies have expressed this. Until recent years, pay increases for service personnel included little or nothing for those with less than two years service —mostly non-careerists. A cheap, short-term labor force represented by the draftee has offered little incentive either to introduce labor-saving devices or to provide substantially better living and recreation facilities in order to attract enlistees.

The move to volunteer forces provides obvious incentives to capital intensification but simultaneously it has created major obstacles to it:

—Personnel costs: dramatically increased direct compensation requirements;

—Life style improvement costs: need for support funds to increase service attractiveness stimulated by years of deterioration of facilities during priority support to Vietnam.

The increased dollar requirements for compensation and support constitute a major resource commitment. As an indication, the "soldier-oriented" Operations and Maintenance (OMA) programs in the fiscal 1973 budget were to cost some $1.2 billion, compared to approximately $800,000,000 in fiscal 1971. The increase is even more dramatic when it is recognized that those funds are applied to a much smaller force. Pay costs per man have more than doubled since the start of the Vietnam War. The average cost per year to pay, feed, clothe, and transport a soldier has increased from about $4,400 in fiscal 1965 to about $9,000 in fiscal 1973. Within a relatively fixed or declining total budget, these increases compete with dollars for materiel—the cost of which is also rapidly increasing. The net effect of these developments is to intensify the need to find ways of using less manpower, and of using it more efficiently.

Attitudes and practices produced by a generation of the

draft contribute additional problems. Probably only the actual experience of losing the draft can provide sufficient impetus for us to overcome certain practices. This will influence not only our approach to such practices as labor-intensive post details but our design of tactical units and the development of employment concepts. Large mass formations will become prohibitively expensive in terms of manpower and the materiel required to support them, and casualties will represent an increasingly greater investment loss—perhaps even an irreplaceable one in the absence of a draft. Our units, our support overhead, and our tactics will need to be designed to use and preserve manpower much more effectively. We did make some adjustment in Vietnam in the realm of tactics, due in part to the unpopularity of the war. Growing public intolerance for U.S. casualties led to extensive use of firepower and mobility in order to reduce the risk of casualties to our ground troops. This was essentially the application of labor-saving techniques, however, not a redesign of organizations along labor-saving lines.

Technical Assimilation

Another factor is the requirement to assimilate the technical advances in materiel that have come as a result of our Vietnam experience. Concurrent with growing pressures to reduce reliance on manpower, we have an embarrassment of riches in new military technology presently in the field. Advances span the range of military activities. Not only do we have a plethora of new type items such as sensors, helicopters, and lasers, but also unparalleled experience in applying many of them in combat situations—for example, our experience in air-ground operations applied in a low-intensity counter-insurgency environment is unequaled. A major challenge is to find appropriate concepts which can enable us to assimilate these advances which resulted from

Vietnam into operational doctrines suitable for mid-intensity conflict such as meeting a Soviet conventional attack on NATO or the prospect of high-intensity conflict involving the use of nuclear weapons. Our principal vehicle for attacking this problem has been the experimental "triple capability" (TRICAP) division at Fort Hood. This organization is explicitly a test bed of the Army's efforts to master Vietnam-generated technology. Perhaps it is a blessing in disguise that this revolutionary effort comes at a time which is also forcing us to re-evaluate manpower practices and policies as well. TRICAP or comparable future test efforts must not only show us how to transfer our technology to the conventional battlefield but how to do it in a way which emphasizes the soldier as a multiplier of machine-generated combat power, not as a substitute for it.

The Army has fine conventional equipment for mid-intensity war today—much of which has not yet been issued to units or assimilated within units—equipment such as the M60A1-M60A2 tanks, the Cobra-TOW combination, and the M551 Sheridan. These possess probably as appropriate and useful mid-intensity capabilities as the Army has ever fielded. Personnel and doctrine may not be as "capable" as the equipment, particularly after a decade of concentration on a totally different type of conflict, fought with different weapons in a different climate against a vastly different Army. An important need is to train and practice to gain full value from our current equipment, not to slight the present in favor of the future as we have often done in the past.

This problem of assimilation of current capabilities is particularly acute in armored units where there has been the most pronounced revolution in capability. Complex equipment has been introduced such as complex turrets requiring very expensive training—mechanical, hydraulic, and electrical turrets of the M60A1, M60A2, and M551. But personnel training and logistics policies necessary to gain full value from the twenty-four-hour per day design capability have lagged.

Without the conceptual changes in support policies—which determine true assimilation—the actual effectiveness of the exotic equipment may be very low. Our habits of the past may inhibit true progress toward capital intensification. We must have the foresight and the candor to acknowledge the broad personnel, training, and logistic requirements of technical assimilation if we are to be truly capital-intensive.

Uniformity of Modernization

A major problem of technical modernization is the rapidly accelerating costs of new systems. Yet in order to maintain adequate capability, we have no choice but to introduce modern equipment and weapons. Our strategic concepts, however, and our basic assumptions concerning ground force employment tend to make the problem even more difficult than it need be. In line with placing a high priority upon hedging against a large conventional contingency, all elements of active and reserve forces are required to be appropriate for the European mid-intensity environment which assumes a sophisticated enemy. As a result we are confronted with modernizing an entire Army when a new system is considered necessary for Europe. Thus we are often in danger of falling between two stools: having insufficient resources to procure a new system across the board, we forego perhaps desirable selective procurement.

We may take three desired major items as examples. These are a new main battle tank, an advanced air defense system, and a follow-on version of the attack helicopter. To develop and try these new items in sufficient quantities for the entire Army is probably prohibitively expensive. But more important it is probably unnecessary as well. Outside of Europe we would not normally expect to operate in a mid-intensity environment. In a previous chapter we have suggested a type force which would be designed for selective employment, with only a portion of our active force dedicated to the large conventional war contingency as a primary mission. Adaptation of our procurement policies to such employment concepts would make possible a more selective capital intensification.

Personnel Quality

There is a real dilemma posed if we become more capital-intensive. The profile of the true volunteer under future conditions is far from clear at this point. In the past, highly skilled individuals were procured by the draft and provided at least partial incentives in the form of "proficiency" pay. The most potent, though unstated, incentive was of course avoidance of service as a rifleman. The termination of the draft, while focusing attention upon the difficulties of attracting infantrymen, affects far more critically our and other services' ability to attract soldiers with advanced skills.

Most attention has focused upon the intelligence level, the "Category", as the primary indicator of quality. Most studies indicate that a volunteer Army will attract relatively more persons of lower intelligence. On the other hand, the reduced requirements for large numbers of unskilled soldiers, which would be a product of capital-intensification, as well as a general reduction in accession requirements as the Army becomes smaller, may permit the Army to be more selective —pick fewer, better men. This would, however, further increase the manpower cost of the force since probably greater incentives would be needed to attract individuals with attractive blue-collar alternatives in civilian life, and a larger percentage of our smaller, capital-intensive Army would be in positions requiring extensive training. This is the ascending spiral of quality referred to above—equipment demanding more sophisticated operator skills which must be better paid, and for whom there must be better equipment. Such is the dilemma of capitalization. Some would argue that this is precisely what we see today, without, unfortunately, the changes in personnel policies required for there to be the more skilled men in units—changes such as better basic MOS training with extensive mid-service upgrading. One solution to the problem, the pluralistic Army, is discussed in Chapter 11.

The "Teeth-To-Tail" Problem

The perception of a fat, support-heavy Army is a common one. To say that we ought to do better with less support is a truism. But determining how much support is enough is a very complex task, as illustrated in the relevant figures. As Figure 8-1 indicates, there are various ways of aggregating a

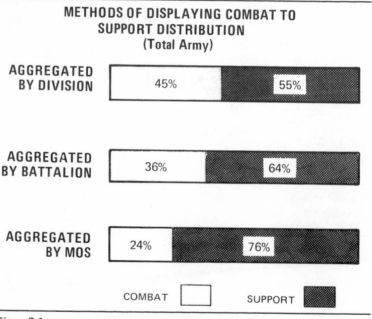

Figure 8-1.

combat-to-support ratio. Figure 8-2 shows that different type elements require different support and should therefore be judged against a different standard. Finally, we see in Table 8-1 that a wartime situation has marked influence. While it would be wrong to assume that increasing levels of support are an unmitigated good, it is equally wrong to condemn a greater support ratio per se. Output must be considered. In some cases, a much greater combat capability payoff has accompanied and results from greater support. It is interesting to compare the equipment density of a 1943 infantry regiment with a 1971 infantry brigade—a comparable unit—as shown in Table 8-2. The substantially smaller brigade has far greater firepower, mobility, and communications with fewer men. This is capital intensification, but a price must be paid in terms of support.

Another way of looking at the problem includes consideration of enhanced weapon lethality. The combat-to-support

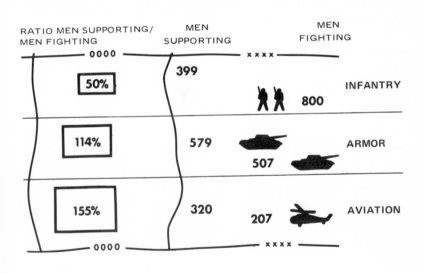

Figure 8-2.

TABLE 8-1
"DIVISION SLICE" INCREASES
DURING WARTIME

	End FY	Army Strength	÷Number of Divisions	='Division Slice"
World War II	1940	267,000	8	34,000
	1945	8,268,000	89	93,000
Korean War	1950	593,000	10	59,000
	1952	1,596,000	20	80,000
Berlin Crisis	1960	873,000	14	62,000
	1962	1,066,000	18	59,000
Vietnam	1965	969,000	16 1/3	59,000
	1969	1,512,000	19 2/3	78,000
Current	1973	791,000	13	61,000

ratio *within* a tank battalion has changed little since World War II, with about ten men in a battalion for every tank. Yet output in terms of tank capability has shown marked improvement, as indicated in Table 8-3.

To say simply that the Army is "fat" is a shallow observation unless explained. But "fat" is relative. In the face of ever-tightening financial and manpower constraints we must continue to improve the combat to combat-support ratio. To begin we must recognize the diverse origins of the "teeth-to-tail" ratio.

Our strategic concepts have had an important influence. These have priority on planning to fight a sustained and

TABLE 8-2
EQUIPMENT DENSITY COMPARISON

	1943 Regiment	1971 Brigade	% Change
Strength	3,135	2,553	− 19
Weapons			
Rifles	2,725	2,119	− 22
Machine Guns	74	129	+ 74
Anti-Tank	153	396	+159
Radios	81	539	+565
Vehicles	205	415	+102

TABLE 8-3

TANK TECHNOLOGY

	1943 M4	1969 M60A1
Crew Size	5	4
Main Gun	76MM	105MM
Types of Ammo	2	4
Rangefinder	None	Optical
Operating Range	100 miles	310 miles
Engagement Range	800 meters	1800 meters

intense conventional war on the World-War-II model. This has led in the past to the inclusion of large numbers of "sustaining" support units in both the active and reserve structure which would be required for long-term conflict. These would come into use only after active forces had been engaged for some months of combat. Quartermaster pipeline and depot units are examples. They are of little direct relevance to in-being combat effectiveness of active combat forces, although they inflate the structure. This particular area has seen substantial improvement in the recent past. Most of the "sustaining" increment units are now in the reserves. However, we are still inclined to retain a high percentage of officers and much of our CONUS base structure as a hedge against large-scale mobilization in the World-War-II model.

Another source of overhead is related to the kind of support considered necessary for the individual soldier. A part of this is an unavoidable consequence of introducing more technical equipment, such as the helicopter, which requires substantial support. In this case, it is a legitimate capital intensification of our forces which has dictated a corresponding adjustment of the support ratio. As Table 8-4 shows, there has been a rough inverse correlation between high levels of support and battle casualties historically. But there are other causes not directly attributable to increased capability. We have tried both to minimize troop casualties

TABLE 8-4
COMBAT/SUPPORT DISTRIBUTION & CASUALTY RATES
(by MOS, in percentages)

	Civil War	WW I	WW II	Korea	VN
Combat	93.2	34.1	36.2	33.0	22.2
Support	6.8	65.9	63.8	67.0	77.8
Battle Casualties*	121.4	83.5	30.6	22.7	19.8
Battle Deaths*	42.9	16.1	9.2	6.4	3.6

*Rates expressed as cases per 1,000 average Army strength per year.

and to provide as high a level of individual services to *all* soldiers as possible in Vietnam. Due in part to the unpopularity of the war, we have enlarged the support "requirements" in pursuit of a fairly comfortable soldier life style.

While the problem of increased non-combat support structure has complex origins, some genuinely derived from more complex equipment but some less defensible on military grounds, it has been exacerbated by the absence of built-in constraints on the proliferation of support requirements. A fixed budget can serve as a gross constraint in this regard, but this was not an operative factor during most of our Vietnam commitment.

Finally, there is the influence of various special interests which exert a large claim on Army resources. It would be neither fair nor accurate to condemn all spokesmen for branches, specialties, and separate projects as blind to the higher interests of the Army in fielding a combat force. But in the aggregate, many of the fences which are erected to protect a fixed level of resources dedicated to various special programs have the effect of putting the cart before the horse. It is estimated that our base structure has a comparatively fixed cost of some $9-13 billion, separate from the cost of combat units per se. A large amount of this is combat-related and otherwise justified. But some of it is not. It exists as a result of genuine yet narrow interests. For example, we have powerful support for our medical program, for our aviation program, for research and development, and for officer schooling programs. Many of these are funded at fixed or growing levels. These claimants compete with the tactical unit for a share of a shrinking resource pie.

Allied Support

A final factor is that of allied support capabilities. Our chief contribution to allies has been in the form of material and technical resources rather than manpower. In the case of Vietnam this has meant support to allied maneuver units and provision of large-scale logistical services to the entire allied force in an underdeveloped physical environment. This has further generated the requirement for support forces within our own structure. Development of a capability to provide assistance to allies with low U.S. personnel involvement and low visibility requires a structure which can provide weapons and firepower effectively beyond the scale needed merely for supporting our own forces.

NEW IMPACT AND DIRECTIONS

Major change in the capital-intensity of our forces may be brought about both by accommodating our structure to new strategic and financial realities and by improving our internal management and training. Much adjustment must occur under the unavoidable impact of rapidly escalating manpower costs.

Two approaches must go hand-in-hand as primary means of achieving essential capital intensity at the individual and unit levels: we must consider our professional, volunteer soldier to be increasingly reliant on machine-generated combat power; and we must correspondingly redesign our units along manpower-saving lines.

The individual foot soldier's traditional role in the past has been "to close with and destroy the enemy" by individual close combat. While close combat will remain as one of his functions, it should be acknowledged as an unlikely one and one inefficient in the use of expensive manpower. Equipment and weaponry now available to today's infantryman such as the M-16 rifle, the claymore mine, the Dragon missile, and the helicopter-borne support available to him, make him potentially far more effective than his World-War-II or Korean War counterpart. The combat soldier cannot be viewed as an always available "grunt" any longer—especially if he is a volunteer whose emoluments now reflect the true costs of military service. He alone can translate the enormous investments we have made, both in dollars and in Vietnam experience, into increased combat effectiveness. This will require and justify far greater and more intensive weapon training for the individual soldier. Professional infantry soldiers must be required to be competent to employ every weapon available within the rifle company. The officers leading such units must be thorough-going experts. The infantry, in other words, must become much more weapons- and equipment-oriented.

Weapons training in basic and advanced individual training should be greatly increased, perhaps even doubled. A standard part of the unit training test should be weapons proficiency—and heavily graded. Every combat arms officers, regardless of assignment, should be given intensive equipment and weapons refresher training annually.

Closely related to this evolution of the role of the soldier must be new approaches to the purpose and employment of the unit. Vietnam experience can help point the way for us. Infantry was used in main force combat there primarily as a finding and fixing force—an anvil against which the enemy could be destroyed by artillery and air power. This role did not, and does not, require infantry-heavy formations. More than anything else it requires mobility, firepower, and communications. The other roles played by infantry in Southeast Asia were as reconnaissance elements in one form or another. Long Range Patrol (LRPs) and Aero-Rifle Platoons performed the function of "finding" the enemy, although "fixing" him was often beyond their means either because they were out of range of fire support or could not be reinforced. This is not to imply that all of our Vietnam innovations are transferable to a mid-intensity conflict—many of them are not. But these type units should be used as models against which our standard infantry unit should be evaluated.

The potent, professional individual soldiers mentioned above should be welded into small, mobile, and highly armed units of the type used so effectively in Vietnam in the air and armored cavalry units. While many of these might be heli-borne, other models of transport such as armored personnel carriers would be used as appropriate to other theaters or other enemies. Infantry units of the future could be substantially smaller than those we have now. This would reflect the greater cost of manpower. The size of an appropriate infantry platoon might be from 20 to 25 men. Companies and battalions could be correspondingly reduced in size.

A final point must be emphasized while discussing the basic soldier. He is too precious a resource to be wasted raking leaves or diverted to other chores, except as is required for the appropriate police of his own or his unit's living area. The combat units of the future should not be used as unskilled labor at the service of others on CONUS posts or elsewhere. These men are going to have to be professionals. They must be used and treated as such.

The total problem cannot be solved at the level of the individual soldier or at the unit level. The combat support and combat service support "tail" must be dealt with also. Efforts must be made to reduce what we now have and to constrain the undisciplined growth of requirements and "sophisticated" new equipment.

One major means by which reduction in non-combat elements can be made is through an honest effort to adapt to the new strategic realities discussed above. We must design our forces for the *most likely* contingencies, not for the *worst case*—a repetition of World War II. It is the "readiness for World War II" syndrome which continues to drive up the officer-to-enlisted ratio and the support structure. We should seek new techniques for the development of lesser cost ways to hedge against the World-War-II contingency. For example, our officer corps and our CONUS base structure should be more narrowly derived from the need to lead and sustain active forces in being, with little redundancy retained for the mobilization contingency beyond that which a modified reserve establishment can furnish.

Closely related to the above is the problem of interjecting more effective constraints on equipment complexity. The "requirements approach" is proving as poor a guide to equipment development as it has as a guide to strategy. We have fielded more sophisticated and complex weapon systems. Unrestrained developmental "wish lists" advanced by competent, capable advocates have produced extraordinarily expensive weapons which become increasingly difficult to operate and maintain. In many cases the world of the user seems to have been overlooked. Unfortunately, the actual users—the battalion and company commanders—cannot represent themselves adequately in the development of many complex projects, especially when there are long-lead times and technical issues involved. Furthermore, the tactical unit has other jobs to perform. But it seems essential that the point of view of the average unit must be brought into the process more effectively if we are to develop more usable equipment.

One technique to involve the true user would be to conduct an anonymous survey of key personnel who must operate the equipment. The survey should assess problems involved in the operation of current equipment as well as solicit unit reaction to proposed developments. To complement these measures, test and evaluation procedures should be reviewed to ensure prototype testing by average soldiers in typical under-resourced units prior to system commitments.

Next, we should modernize selectively, rather than attempt to fit most of our structure into a single mold. In accordance with the corps type force suggested earlier we should procure advanced equipment against the needs of the appropriate contingency force. Obviously for many if not most items, all units throughout the Army will be similarly equipped. But for high value specialized end items, great selectivity is in order for tailored task forces. Three key systems portray the potential of selective equipping:

Advanced Armed Helicopters are vital in Middle East and European contingencies but are of negligible marginal advantage in low-intensity areas. Procurement should therefore be limited to those needed to support the contingency forces tailored for those mid-intensity environments—perhaps one-half of the force.

Advanced Air Defense Systems are required only against a sophisticated enemy air threat. For a three-corps Army, one to two "Corps packages" should be retained to support deployment to mid-intensity areas or special cases of potential air threat. All units would retain standard "cheap" defensive capability such as Chapparel and Redeye.

Advanced Main Battle Tanks would be procured on a similar basis. Adequate capability for most non-European contingencies can be achieved with improved standard models. Packages of highly sophisticated armor would be procured solely for forces dedicated to a NATO type scenario.

These illustrations suggest that acceptance of task force specialization reduces costs by limiting issue to relatively few units. This would have the added advantage of maintaining an advanced "state of the art" across a wide range.

The final major reform suggested is one which is basic. We must learn again that unit integrity is the heart and soul of the Army. We have been trading off unit viability for too long. It is tacitly accepted, even by many combat commanders, that the understrength TOE (Table of Organization and Equipment) units are commonplace. This must stop, for it erodes the fighting capability of the Army and demonstrates to all that our priorities are in need of adjustment. We are being less than forthright and less than professionally conscientious when we fail to put unit viability first. We are losing a great deal when we convince ourselves and others that understrength and incomplete units are acceptable, even when we know that they do not meet our own stated standards.

We should make every effort to keep the average "present for duty" strength of our combat battalions at 100%. This would be a very important move both symbolically and in terms of lower-echelon morale. It would demonstrate that our priorities are in the proper order and that the structure of our Army is truly determined by the combat requirement. The demonstration of this, plus the increased confidence in mission capability it would give to the troop units, would pay large dividends.

Obviously there are problems in implementing such a policy, chief of which is short-tour generated personnel turbulence. As this decreases due to the removal of forces from Vietnam and recent reductions in the Korean garrison, improvements should become feasible. The actual numbers at issue are small in comparison to total Army strength, for we have comparatively few combat battalions. But these are the cutting edge of the Army, and its soul. They deserve far higher resource priority.

Chapter 9

THE COSTS OF AN ARMY FOR
COALITION SECURITY

Resource Implications of Strategic Concepts. In the preceding chapter we have dealt with a range of new concepts and their application to key policy areas. The resource implications of these concepts have not been addressed explicitly. Yet in the actual world of budgets and programs, all innovations and changes have price tags.

What would it cost to reshape the Army along the lines suggested in preceding chapters? Strategic concepts must be attainable within reasonable resource levels. Those under discussion obviously have significant cost implications when translated into the men and materiel which must give substance to them. Several problems arise when trying to assess these, however.

First, there are almost limitless numbers of different ways to put together as complex an organization as an Army, even within a single set of assumptions. To take one small example, we could opt for several different mixes of divisions each with a corresponding price tag.

AUTHORS' NOTE: We are indebted to the assistance of Maxwell Thurman in developing our costing methodology.

[147]

Second, the true cost, in absolute terms, of military forces is in many respects virtually impossible to obtain. Much of the current structure has already been paid for. Much of this would serve under new strategic concepts as well. For example, a firing range built years ago would serve to train soldiers in support of a containment strategy or a coalition strategy equally well.

And third, actual practice over the years has consisted of making frequent incremental changes in response to required program adjustments. Our cost factors which we associate with various resources therefore do not necessarily reflect the true cost of building a force "from scratch."

While we must recognize these problems, we need not allow them to prevent us from making some useful general assessments which are reasonably accurate. This is particularly true if we are content to be fairly confident in general, and be less concerned about accuracy in detail. While forces can be shaped in a wide variety of ways, we can look at several of various sizes which are representative of the type desired, and significantly different from the current force to demonstrate the larger cost implications. Likewise, the existence of prior investment and cost factors derived from incremental changes need not bother us unduly. This is because as a practical matter we would never start over from scratch to build a different force but would simply modify the existing one. So in effect we would in large measure still be making incremental changes.

What we will illustrate here are the potential resource implications in major areas of moving from a "containment" force to a "contingency" force of comparable size. We shall do this by comparing the force programed for fiscal 1973 with a hypothetical new force designed in accordance with different assumptions. The variation in assumptions and the cost implications will be briefly assessed in the six major budgetary categories. Several years would be required to implement our proposals, therefore we are more realistically comparing the fiscal 1973 status quo with a fiscal 1975 projection of our Ready Army.

At the outset the reader is reminded of the overall purpose of this effort—to explore new approaches to security, especially as they affect the Army. The aim is not to advocate larger or smaller forces as being a desirable end in itself, nor to find a route to achieving savings. We feel that the latter would in particular place the cart before the horse. Any major cost differentials between the new type force which we have described and the one currently programed should be considered as implications of more fundamental judgments concerning strategy and our security interests rather than as indices for assessing the overall desirability of these judgments. Our purpose in developing a rough set of cost estimates is to demonstrate that the coalition approach to security, which we feel is necessary, can be translated into specific enough program guidance to make it a useful conceptual alternative for force design. Emphasis should not be placed upon the dollar figures in moving toward a different type force, but attention should instead be focused upon the new departures and concepts which they represent.

We would likewise introduce a cautionary word in connection with the Army force which we posit as a model —especially with regard to the number of divisions. There is nothing magic about the various sizes of the force which we use as a basis for discussion. Indeed, we wish it were possible to discuss a new type force without numbers of units. Unfortunately, that is not the case when dollars are to be considered. That is one of the important disciplinary effects of attempting to make an honest assessment of the resource implications of a new strategy. Specific assumptions cannot be avoided. We want to make it clear that we are proposing neither an increase to fifteen divisions nor a reduction to eleven or nine divisions. Rather, we are attempting to demonstrate a type force which in its overall design is consistent with the demands and conditions of a new era which is coming fast upon us. We would not argue that other division mixes or numbers of divisions might be more suitable. There is much room for honest professional disagreement over both the need for forces and the degree of risk which should willingly be accepted. We would note that should the general contingency approach be taken, great flexibility exists in modifying the force structure—indeed, the flexibility would be far greater than our current approach provides.

Assumptions Underlying Costing

We have discussed new concepts and their application in various areas of policy in preceding chapters. But in order to make reasonably precise costing estimates, these must be translated into a set of more specific assumptions which are of sufficient explicitness to provide quantitative as opposed to qualitative guidance. Our basic assumption is that forces needed for coalition security—primarily ground force requirements for NATO defense (sufficient and survivable)—integrated with mobilization capabilities provided by our reserve forces concept, and supported by a stand-by draft, combine to require an active Army of substantial size and capability. We have selected type Ready Armies of 15, 13, 11, and 9 active divisions as representative of alternative Army forces for fiscal 1975 (Cases A-D). We recognize that the evolving world situation may vary the need for active ground forces. For example, successful MBFR negotiations may eventually permit the reduction of ground forces in Europe. To demonstrate the effect of just such a situation we have developed a Ready Army (Case D) composed of 9 active divisions. Finally we portray two levels of reserve mobilization capability—"normal" reserves (expandable to 5 divisions by M + 90 and 15 divisions by M + 180) and "augmented" reserves (expandable to 10 divisions by M + 90 and 20 divisions by M + 180).

THE READY ARMY

(1) *Force Composition:* Current force structuring practice divides army forces into three groupings: the combat division (16,000 men) supported by Initial Support Increments (16,000 men in units providing the combat and service support required during the first sixty days of combat) and Sustaining Support Increments (16,000 men in units providing the combat and service support required for sustained combat operations). We assume that each active army division will be supported by one support increment in the active army and one support increment in a modified reserve structure. NATO forces are reinforced by one additional support increment in Cases A, B, and C. Two additional increments are required in Case D to offset reductions in organizational support which would accompany reduction of division forces in order to enhance the survivability of the force. The forces would be disposed as indicated in Table 9-1.

(2) *Force Size:* Approximately 688,000 to 930,000 military personnel dependent upon 9-to-15 division capability selected. A stand-by draft would be maintained to include classification and mobilization designation of personnel.

(3) *Force Readiness:* All active units would be maintained at 100% manning of structure at all times. Funds and time devoted to training would be augmented with at least a twofold increase in scheduled field operations. Transition to a Ready Army would occur over two to three years in order to reduce personnel turbulence and degradation of unit readiness.

(4) *Active Forces:* The active divisions would be fully equipped and provided sufficient personnel and equipment support to ensure 95% equipment availability at all times. Units would be equipped commensurate with the anticipated threat. Thus, units assigned to a Heavy Corps in Europe would be provided the most sophisticated mechanized warfare equipment obtainable; units earmarked for Asian operations would be provided less sophisticated equipment suitable for the expected threat (tanks and air defense). No division sets of equipment would be pre-positioned overseas.

TABLE 9-1

FORCE COMPOSITION[a]

	Case A		Case B	
	Divisions	*Support Increments*	*Divisions*	*Support Increments*
1 Heavy Corps (Europe)	5	6	5	6
1 Heavy Corps (CONUS)	5	5	5	5
1 Light Corps (CONUS)	5	5	3	3
Totals	15	16 [b]	13	14[c]

	Case C		Case D	
	Divisions	*Support Increments*	*Divisions*	*Support Increments*
1 Heavy Corps (Europe)	5	6	3	5
1 Heavy Corps (CONUS)	3	3	3	3
1 Light Corps (CONUS)	3	3	3	3
Totals	11	12[d]	9	11[e]

a. Excludes nondivisional Special Mission Brigades in Berlin, Alaska, and Panama.
b. 14 additional Support Increments would be formed after mobilization.
c. 12 additional Support Increments would be formed after mobilization.
d. 10 additional Support Increments would be formed after mobilization.
e. 7 additional Support Increments would be formed after mobilization.

Logistic Planning Guidance for Active Forces

Active forces would be provided sufficient war reserve stocks to provide for 150 days of combat in Europe for the Europe Corps reinforced by the Heavy Corps from CONUS. The requirement varies dependent upon the number of divisions in the Corps (10 divisions in Cases A and B, 8 divisions in Case C, and 6 divisions in Case D). War reserve stocks for all other contingencies (the Mid-East or Asia) would be sufficient for 150 days of combat for up to 3 divisions in Cases B, C and D, 5 divisions in Case A. Deployment capability in all cases would obviously be dependent upon the adequacy of strategic mobility assets. We considered analysis of these to be beyond the scope of this effort.

(5) *Reserve Forces:* The active Ready Army would be supported by a sizable reserve in the event of mobilization. As discussed in Chapter 6, we believe that a combination of trained cadre and intensive post-mobilization training will provide sufficient capability. Two levels of reserve support, normal and augmented, are portrayed in Table 9-2 and explanatory footnotes.

(6) *Force Build-up Scenario:* The combination of active and reserve force capabilities which we propose provides a broad range of mobilization alternatives. The force build-up concept is illustrated in schematic form in Table 9-3 (p. 158).

The alternative mobilization capabilities indicated in Table 9-3 provide a wide range of alternative capabilities for the support of coalition security operations. For example, Case B augmented reserves should permit support of a fully "survivable" and "sufficient" NATO commitment—5 divisions in Europe backed up by a 5-division heavy "reinforcing" corps from CONUS and supported by 10 reserve divisions on M + 90. This should provide for 20 U.S. divisions supporting NATO shortly after M + 90.

(7)) *Aide to Allies:* Military support to allies would be maintained at presently programed levels—$1.4 billion per year primarily to Republic of Vietnam, South Korea, and Thailand. The nature of assistance and recipient countries would vary. It would remain a major defense program, however.

(8) *Safeguard (ABM):* Safeguard program costs are in a dynamic state as a result of the SALT negotiations. Therefore, the costing methodology adapted herein deletes Safeguard costs associated with the fiscal 1973 budget and treats these costs as a constant throughout all calculations. Whatever the final costs are determined to be, we assume that they will apply equally to all of our alternative force calculations.

TABLE 9-2

RESERVE FORCES CAPABILITY

Alternative 1: Ready Army (Case C)—Normal Reserves	*Personnel*

Combat Forces

5 Div at cadre strength in Reserves @ 2,000 officers and enlisted cadre (Div to Bn Staffs, senior NCOs)[a]	= 10,000
10 Combat Training Commands @ 4,000 men Train 5 Div with pre-M-day cadre in 60 days[b] Train 10 Div with no pre-M-day cadre in 90 days	= 40,000
2 Combat Replacement Training Centers @ 4,000 men[c] Train 20,000 combat replacements per 60 days	= 8,000

Support Forces

10 Support Increments at cadre strength in Reserves @ 2,000 officers and enlisted cadre[d]	= 20,000
15 Support Training Commands @ 2,000 men Train 10 Support Increments with pre-M-day cadre in 60 days Train 15 Support Increments with no pre-M-day cadre in 90 days	= 30,000
1 Support Replacement Training Center @ 4,000 men Trains 10,000 support replacements per 60 days	= 4,000
2 Support Increments maintained full strength in Reserves @ 16,000 men[e]	= 32,000
Administration and Overhead	6,000
Total Personnel	150,000

Equipment Required[f]

ll Active Div + 5 Reserve Div = 16 Division sets for issue by M + 90
Long lead time equipment would be procured and stored for issue on M + 120
Post M + 150 equipment would be provided from post M-day production

Mobilization Schedule[g]

M +   30: Start Training
M +   90: + 5 Div, 10 SI prepared for deployment
M + 120: + 5 Div, 5 SI prepared for deployment
M + 180: + 5 Div, 10 SI prepared for deployment

Alternative 2: Ready Army (Case C)—Augmented Reserves	*Personnel*

Combat Forces

| 10 Div at cadre strength in Reserves @ 2,000 officers and enlisted cadre (Div to Bn Staffs, senior NCOs) | = 20,000 |
| 10 Combat Training Commands @ 4,000 men
Train 10 Div with pre-M-day cadre in 60 days
Train 10 Div with no pre-M-day cadre in 90 days | = 40,000 |

TABLE 9-2 (continued)

2 Combat Replacement Training Centers @ 4,000 men	= 8,000
Train 20,000 combat replacements per 60 days	

Support Forces

15 Support Increments at cadre strength in Reserves	= 30,000
@ 2,000 meh officers and enlisted cadre	
15 Support Training Commands @ 2,000 men	= 30,000
Train 10 Support Increments with pre-M-day cadre in 60 days	
Train 15 Support Increments with no pre-M-day cadre in 90 days	
1 Support Replacement Training Center @ 4,000 men	= 4,000
Trains 10,000 support replacements per 60 days	
3 Support Increments maintained full strength in Reserves	= 48,000
@16,000 men	

Administration and Overhead	8,000
Total Personnel	188,000

Equipment Required

11 Active Div + 10 Reserve Div = 21 Division sets on hand for issue by M + 90
All issue after M + 150 from post M-day production

Mobilization Schedule[h]

M + 30: Start training
M + 90: + 10 Div, 15 SI prepared for deployment
M + 180: + 10 Div, 15 SI prepared for deployment
M + 270: + 10 Div, 15 SI prepared for deployment

a. Cadre-size based on World-War-II experience. Office, Chief of Military History, has selected the experience of the 65th Infantry Division in 1943 as the case study in mobilization and training of division-size units. The 65th Division was provided a cadre of 192 officers and 1,400 enlisted men 1 to 4 weeks prior to arrival of the newly inducted untrained soldiers. The division underwent a 38-week training program—14 weeks basic and individual training, 12 weeks unit training (to regimental level) and 12 weeks combined arms training. The cadre for the 5 quick-reaction reserve divisions which we propose would be maintained in the command and staff positions which they would occupy in the event of mobilization. They would train in these positions for at least one month annually in conjunction with the active army.

b. Training of the reserve divisions would be conducted by Combat Training Commands organized, trained, and equipped to provide highly sophisticated, capital-intensive, imaginative individual and unit training. We believe that these Combat Training Commands, provided the resources (money, men, and training area) and the knowledge of job tasks and educational techniques acquired since World War II, can achieve revolutionary improvements in individual and unit training. Following normal cadre procedures—cadre formed after M-day from the State Militia (old National Guard) and the active army—it should be possible to train draftee to division level in 12 weeks (approximately 1/3 of World-War-II

TABLE 9-2 (continued)

period). Where the leadership of the division (division to battalion level) has had the opportunity to train together extensively in peacetime, we believe that the response time can be reduced to 8 weeks. This is a key assumption which should be verified by test. We see the critical factor in the drastic compression of training time to be physical conditioning. Eight weeks is probably the absolute minimum time.

c. Combat Replacement Training Centers would train individual and small units replacements in 8 weeks, using the same advanced techniques as indicated above.

d. The combat divisions would have to be provided essential combat and combat-service support—one or more Support Increments per division. Rapid-response Support Increments would be provided peacetime cadre to permit creation of deployable units in 8 weeks. Many of the skills required in the Support Increments would be civilian-related, with individuals assigned to units after mobilization based upon testing and classification of personnel in a stand-by selective service system operating during peacetime.

e. Two full-strength, trained Support Increments are maintained in the reserves to support active army units when they deploy. These units would be prepared for deployment by M + 60. Other support requirements for active army units would be met by maintaining a support reserve training base greater than a combat reserve training base—15 Support Training Commands to 10 Combat Training Commands production capacity.

f. All equipment required for units deployable by M + 90 would be provided and maintained for issue during the period M + 30 to M + 90. Long lead time equipment would be provided and maintained for units deployable M + 90 to M + 150. The only items to be stockpiled prior to M-day would be those items which could not be provided from a warm production base by M + 120, assuming production commencing M + 30. All equipment need not be new. Serviceable "long lead time" equipment recently phased out of the active Army would be retained for issue to the 5 divisions and 5 Support Increments ready at M + 120. All equipment (end items, ammunition, etc.) requirements after M + 150 would be met from post-M-day production.

g. The detailed mobilization schedule for a "normal" reserve force would be:

M-day	Mobilization—activation of stand-by draft
M + 30	Units commence training
M + 60	2 Support Increments deployable in support of active army
M + 90	5 combat divisions, 10 Support Increments prepared for deployment (units with pre-M-day cadre, 60 days training)
M + 120	5 combat divisions, 5 Support Increments prepared for deployment (units with post-M-day cadre from active army and Militia, 90 days training commencing M + 30)
M + 150	No output
M + 180	5 combat divisions, 10 Support Increments prepared for deployment (units which entered training centers on M + 90—upon deployment of rapid-response units, 90 days training commencing M + 30)

TABLE 9-2 (continued)

h. The detailed mobilization schedule for an "augmented" reserve force would be:

M-day	Mobilization—activation of stand-by draft
M + 30	Units commence training
M + 60	3 Support Increments deployable in support of active army
M + 90	10 combat divisions, 15 Support Increments prepared for deployment (units with pre-M-day cadre, 60 days training)
M + 150	No output
M + 180	10 combat divisions, 15 Support Increments prepared for deployment (units with post-M-day cadre from active army and Militia, 90 days training commencing M + 90)

Considerations

The plan shown in Table 9-3 illustrates several mobilization alternatives. It provides force build-up scenarios in accordance with the strategic and employment concepts which have been discussed in previous chapters. But within the framework represented, additional variations are possible. Both the number of active divisions maintained in the base Army and the rate at which reserve elements are trained and deployed can be varied. All variations obviously have resource implications. The incremental cost of each additional active division must include personnel and operating costs as well as procurement funds for new equipment and war reserve consumption-stocks. The price of changing the rate of force build-up is more complex, requiring re-calculation of the cost of war reserve and production base support for each variation. A key element to be resolved prior to adoption of any general scenario is the level of forces required at about M + 90. With our approach concerning reserve mobilization, it seems that production of 5 to 10 divisions in 90 days after initiation of the draft is as much as can reasonably be accomplished starting from cadre to build combat-ready units. Active force availability must be tailored in order that, when added to the 5 to 10 reserve divisions, a sufficient total force exists at the critical point. After M + 90 more flexibility exists to vary the rate of unit formation and thus the total number of divisions available for deployment.

TABLE 9-3

ALTERNATIVE MOBILIZATION CAPABILITIES

Active Divisions	+	Reserve Divisions	=	(Cumulative Total)	
	M-day	M + 90	M + 120	M + 150	M + 180
Ready Army Case A Normal reserves	15	+ 5= (20)	+ 5= (25)	+ 0= (25)	+ 5= (30)
Ready Army Case A Augmented reserves	15	+10= (25)	+ 0= (25)	+0= (25)	+10= (35)
Ready Army Case B Normal reserves	13	+ 5= (18)	+ 5= (23)	+ 0= (23)	+ 5= (28)
Ready Army Case B Augmented reserves	13	+10= (23)	+ 0= (23)	+ 0= (23)	+10= (35)
Ready Army Case C Normal reserves	11	+ 5= (16)	+ 5= (21)	+ 0= (21)	+ 5= (26)
Ready Army Case C Augmented reserves	11	+10= (21)	+ 0= (21)	+ 0= (21)	+10= (31)
Ready Army Case D Normal reserves	9	+ 5= (14)	+ 5= (19)	+ 0= (19)	+ 5= (24)
Ready Army Case D Augmented reserves	9	+10= (19)	+ 0= (19)	+ 0= (19)	+10= (29)

The concept presented represents a demanding requirement for a comparatively small active force which must
provide the bulk of initial units and manage the reserve
build-up. Here we must consider the relationship between
modification of the institutional structure (to be discussed in
Chapter 11 as a pluralistic Army) and force composition. We
consider that the Army can husband its manpower suitable
for combat elements by greater reliance upon women and
civilians in support elements. This will be an important means
of achieving the kind of combat capability we believe

necessary, but which a volunteer environment makes more difficult to achieve. We also consider that the terms of mobilization would ensure provision of selected officer and NCO cadre from the National Guard (State Militia), as discussed earlier in Chapter 6. Properly trained, these individuals would relieve a portion of the mobilization burden from active Army personnel.

Resource Comparison and Implications

With this rather lengthy set of specific assumptions, we can observe some significant areas of difference between the current Army and four representative forces suitable for coalition security operations in fiscal 1975. These forces are the 15-division Ready Army, Case A; the 13-division Ready Army, Case B; the 11-division Ready Army, Case C; and the 9-division Ready Army, Case D. Characteristics of these forces are summarized in Table 9-4.

It is evident that some cost implications accompany our force structuring assumptions. The range of difference is most evident when we examine each of the major Army appropriation categories in more detail. All costs are displayed in fiscal 1975 dollars.

Military Personnel, Army (MPA)–Current Force FY 1975 dollars: $8.2 Bil; Ready Army 15 Div: $8.5 Bil; 13 Div: $7.8 Bil; 11 Div: $7.3 Bil; 9 Div: $6.8 Bil. These computations exclude retired pay.

The reduction in MPA in the 11 and 9 division forces is caused primarily by the decrease in personnel—from 841,000 in FY 1973 to 762,000 (11 Div), 688,000 (9 Div) military personnel in FY 1975-76. Adjustment has been made for 3% cost-of-living increase per year but not for other general pay increases. Additional savings would be generated as personnel turbulence is reduced (fewer personnel moves).

Operations and Maintenance Army (OMA)–Current Force FY 1975
dollars: $7.3 Bil; Ready Army 15 Div: $7.6 Bil; 13 Div: $7.3 Bil;
11 Div: $7.0 Bil; 9 Div: $6.7 Bil. Cost-of-living growth of 3% per
year is included in the calculation but other pay raises for the
civilian work force are excluded.

OMA expenditures remain relatively high due to the great
increase in funds allocated for improved, more intensive unit
training and for maintenance of enhanced professionalism in
Army units. Current OMA training and maintenance costs per
active division are approximately $9,000,000 per year. This
would be increased to approximately $30,000,000 per year
for each division and support increment. Improved training
would include more field training exercises at all levels
–platoon to corps–with considerable expansion of requirements for firing of weapons and for the conduct of extended

TABLE 9-4

COMPARISON CURRENT FORCE TO FY 1975 READY ARMY–
CASE A-CASE D

CAPABILITY SUMMARY–READY ARMY					
	FY 1973	*Case A 15 Divisions*	*Case B 13 Divisions*	*Case C 11 Divisions*	*Case D 9 Divisions*
Military personnel	841,000	930,000	850,000	762,000	688,000
Direct and indirect hire civilian personnel	438,000	448,000	440,000	425,000	400,000
Reserve Component paid drill strength	660,000	150,000	150,000	150,000	150,000
Active Divisions and necessary supporting units	13	15	13	11	9
Reserve Component divisions[a]	8	5 (at M + 90)	5 (at M + 90)	5 (at M + 90)	5 (at M + 90)
Safeguard sites (excluded from costing)	2	2	2	2	2

TABLE 9-4 (continued)

FISCAL SUMMARY (in billions)
Costs in FY 1975 Dollars
(Rounded to nearest 100 million)

Appropriation Category	FY 1973 President's¹ Budget Force	Case A 15 Divisions	Case B 13 Divisions	Case C 11 Divisions	Case D 9 Divisions
Military personnel, Army	8.2	8.5	7.8	7.3	6.8
Operations and maintenance	7.3	7.6	7.3	7.0	6.7
Procurement, equipment and material	3.5	3.7	3.3	2.8	2.7
Research and development	2.2	2.3	2.2	2.0	2.1
Military construction	1.1	.8	.7	.7	.6
Reserve components	1.8	.8	.8	.8	.8
Totals	24.1ᵇ	23.7	22.1	20.6	19.7
	− 1.7 Est. Safeguard Costs				
FY 1973 Army budget in FY 1975 dollars less Safeguard	22.4				

a. "Normal" Reserve option for Ready Army (5 Divisions at M + 90).
b. Excludes $.399 Bil. in Army Family Housing in DOD accounts.

strategic deployment maneuvers. We would hope that all combat or combat support units would spend 90 to 120 days per year in a field operational environment. To effect this, annual training funds would be increased.

Enhanced professionalism would be achieved through increased civilian hire for menial post housekeeping chores, thus releasing more soldiers for field operations. Presumably there would be also reduced individual training costs as the annual turnover of the force diminishes with the impact of volunteer accessions and improved re-enlistment rates.

Procurement Equipment and Material Army (PEMA)–Current Force FY 1975 dollars: $2.8 Bil; Ready Army 15 Div: $3.7 Bil; 13 Div: $3.3 Bil; 11 Div: $2.8 Bil; 9 Div: $2.7 Bil. (not including Safeguard costs).

Some savings are achieved in the PEMA account for the 11 and 9 division forces as the reserve mobilization force requirements are reassessed. Rather than continually equip some 21 divisions (active and reserve) for a replay of World War II, we have proposed a range of active division forces backed up by 5 divisions by M + 90 days with subsequent force equipping from a warm production base. Equipment would be maintained for these (active + 5) divisions rather than 21 (13 active + 8 reserve) divisions at present in Cases C and D.

Any cost savings achieved by reductions in the number of divisions required to be equipped prior to M + 90 are partially compensated for by the increased costs of maintaining a credible ready warm production base. We assume opening of major production facilities by M + 30 with complete equipping of 5 divisions per 30 days by M + 150.

Cases A and B (15 and 13 division forces) provide for 23 and 25 divisions (active and reserve) prior to M + 150. Additional equipment must be purchased for these divisions. To reduce the annual cost of this equipment, we spread the purchase over 3 years–FY 1974 to 1977.

Research Development Test and Engineering (RDTE)–Current Force FY 1975 dollars: $1.8 Bil; Ready Army 15 Div: $2.3 Bil; 13 Div: $2.2 Bil; 11 Div: $2.0 Bil; 9 Div: $2.1 Bil. (excluding Safeguard).

There would be a relative increase in R&D expenditure compared to the size of the total budget as the Army is reduced in size. This reflects greater Army reliance on an aggressive R&D program. Emphasis should be placed on workable, low-cost "product improvements" in lieu of state-of-the-art advances. Further R&D should be directed at the engineering of the production base in recognition of the increased reliance on maintenance of a quickly responsive production capability. An annual 4% cost growth is assumed.

Military Construction Army (MCA)–Current Force FY 1975 dollars: $.680 Bil; Ready Army 15 Div: $.830 Bil; 13 Div: $.710 Bil; 11 Div: $.675 Bil; 9 Div: $.640 Bil. (excluding Safeguard).

MCA is reduced as the Safeguard system is completed but earlier year initiatives to improve troop housing, bachelor, and dependent housing are maintained. For the 15-division force, an additional $100,000,000 per year for two years will be required to provide stationing facilities in CONUS for the two new active divisions. An additional $80,000,000 per year is required for facilities for the 15-divison force, $50,000,000 for the 11-division force, $35,000,000 for the 9-division force. MCA remains a major program oriented to improvement of garrison living conditions within the Army.

Reserve Components–Current Force FY 1975 dollars: $1.8 Bil; Ready Army 15 Div: $.800 Bil; 13 Div: $.800 Bil; 11 Div: $.800 Bil; 9 Div: $.800 Bil (see Table 9-5).

A major cost reduction is caused by the reduction in the size of the reserves from 660,000 paid drill strength. We expect, however, a more skilled reserve able to train rapidly new units in the event of mobilization. This infers a higher

TABLE 9-5
COST SUMMARY
(Excludes Safeguard in all cases)
FY 1975 Dollars (in billions)

Summation FY 1973 Force	Total FY 1975 dollars	$22.4
Ready Army 15 Div	Total FY 1975 dollars	$23.7
Ready Army 13 Div	Total FY 1975 dollars	$22.1
Ready Army 11 Div	Total FY 1975 dollars	$20.6
Ready Army 9 Div	Total FY 1975 dollars	$19.7

density of quality skilled personnel and provision of considerable sophisticated training aids to the training divisions. These improvements should cost approximately $350,000,000 per year. Reflecting this cost increase and a 3% cost-of-living increase, we have almost doubled per capita expenditures for reserve personnel.

Substantial savings are not achievable without acceptance of reduced active force capability, a need for greater mobilization warning, and dependence on rapid industrial conversion to armaments production. We believe that these may be reasonable provided there is honest improvement in the organization, training, and equipping of residual forces. That is an Army problem of internal reduction and improvement. More fundamental, however, we believe that the price of not changing is potentially greater than can be portrayed by dollar figures, by failure to reshape Army forces appropriate to a post-containment period of foreign policy.

As we have stated several times above, we do not presume that any one force we portray is the sole feasible force for the conduct of coalition security operations. We have

TABLE 9-6

COST ESTIMATES*

Ready Army	Number of Divisions	Annual Cost FY 1975 (in billions)	
		1973 Dollars	1975 Dollars
Case A normal reserves	15 + 5, 5, 0, 5	22.5	23.7
Case A augmented reserves	15 + 10, 0, 0, 10	22.6	23.9
Case B normal reserves	13 + 5, 5, 0, 5	21.3	22.1
Case B augmented reserves	13 + 10, 0, 0, 10	21.4	22.3
Case C normal reserves	11 + 5, 5, 0, 5	19.1	20.6
Case C augmented reserves	11 + 10, 0, 0, 10	19.3	20.8
Case D normal reserves	9 + 5, 5, 0, 5	18.4	19.7
Case D augmented reserves	9 + 10, 0, 0, 10	18.6	19.9
FY 1973 Status Quo (less Safeguard)	13 + 8	21.1	22 4

*Modest support for allies has been included.
Safeguard excluded in all computations.

portrayed alternative division forces with a mobilization of roughly 10 divisions per 60 days commencing M + 90 days (Table 9-3 on Ready Army normal reserves). There are other force structures which would stress augmented reserves indicated in Table 9-3.

Very rough annual cost estimates for all these various forces are as indicated in Table 9-6. (Assumptions such as increased active unit training, improved professionalism, expanded R&D, rapid mobilization training, and variable equipping of units to meet alternate threats remain constant.)

Conclusion

Perhaps the most significant conclusion to be drawn from the brief analysis of the cost implications is that a new force of the type suggested (Ready Army) appears to be within the range of resources which we may reasonably expect to be available for fielding a capable Army in the post-Vietnam future. The Ready Army can provide a viable force in accordance with the strategic concepts developed earlier in support of coalition security. We believe that it would be difficult to demonstrate that current strategic and employment concepts are equally flexible and responsive.

Part III

RESPONDING TO SOCIAL CHANGE

Chapter 10

INSTITUTIONAL ADAPTATION

Thus far, our focus has been on Army adjustment to evolving demands on military capability—new missions which the Army may be called upon to perform. This ordering is proper, for the Army's very existence is based upon the nature of immediate or potential threats to the security of the nation. The structure, composition, and combat readiness of the Army must be such that needs for military land power can be met. It is understandable and desirable that national concern—civilian leadership, the Congress, and the press—focuses on continuing issues of resource allocation to address potential demands for the use of American ground power. Issues such as the numbers of men in divisions, the quality and quantity of tanks or helicopters or trucks are frequently debated, and rightfully so, for they involve national resources and they are amenable to reasonably knowledgeable discussion by concerned neophytes. The budget process provokes annual debate of these kinds of questions.

Unfortunately, external review seldom focuses Army attention on other aspects of military readiness. Allocation of resources to meet probable challenges is only a portion of the overall problem of Army readiness. Equally important are the internal policies and practices which govern the actual day-to-day use of Army resources. These internal practices will govern the true capabilities of the Ready Army we have discussed in Parts I and II. Issues such as styles of leadership, integrity, discipline, fairness of opportunity, and central-ization of authority are crucial to actual military ability but they are elusive policy issues. Seldom quantifiable, they are often decided by soft data, subjective impressions, and the intuition of the professional practitioner. Introspective review of these types of internal issues is rarely stimulated by civilian leadership or the Congress, save when there is a crisis of such magnitude that serious error is overtly evident—crises such as My Lai, the Service Clubs scandals, and senior officer impropriety. This delegation of responsibility for continuing review from national authority to the military services doubtlessly reflects both a reasonable presumption of pro-fessional competence and credibility and a realization that there are no ready management tools such as annual budgetary review available in such subjective areas of professional ethos. Whatever the motivation, the result is the same. The Army is expected to continually review and validate or modify its professional practices.

The Army has not responded fully to the dual challenges of internal review and modification. As a large organization struggling to expand for and then contract from Vietnam, and facing interminable haggling over the budgetary process, the Army has found it difficult to respond to several serious challenges posed by our changing domestic environment. These problems will not be solved by others. They require the most difficult kinds of response for a large organization —internal discipline and self-generated change. The difficulty is compounded by the fundamental questioning implicit in several basic philosophical issues facing the Army. Issues such as: preservation of values, primacy of combat readiness, professional integrity, acceptance of diversity, equality of treatment of individuals, uniformity of authority, avoidance of individual underemployment, emphasis on field environment, maintenance of discipline and leadership, and decentralization. There is a pressing need for the formulation of agreed conceptual guidelines to direct policies relating to these issues. This chapter will propose such conceptual guidelines appropriate to a Ready Army serving a changing America.

Each of the basic issues facing the Army must be weighed in the context of the evolutionary change in personal values of most Americans in the face of increased affluence. Stimulated by basic questioning of the purposes and limitations of American power applied overseas as exemplified in Vietnam, and by lurking awareness that our environment may not be able to support globally the life style we advocate almost as a tenet of faith in America, there is a wholly refreshing and healthy self-questioning occurring throughout the United States. Stimulated by the mass media, there is a new candor emerging in the American consciousness.

The candor is reflected in increasing concern about living up to the declared standards of the Declaration of Independence and the Constitution. Basic questions are now being addressed such as: Is there to be *true* equality among races and sexes? What are the minimum prerequisites of opportunity for all Americans in terms of satisfaction of physical wants and education? What are the limits of personal freedom imposed by decreasing availability of resources or by the demands of serving the nation? If it is to remain a viable force the Army must be prepared to address honestly and candidly questions such as these as they relate to maintenance of ground power.

The difficulty of determining the nature of the Army's response to these problems is increased by the compounding effects of science and technology on the conduct of war. We have adapted well to evolutionary change in the weaponry of ground combat. There has been traditional reluctance to assimilate new weapons—epitomized by the agonizing demise of horse cavalry prior to World War II—but the principles of command have always remained essentially unchanged. Vietnam has ushered in a new and unsettling dimension of science and technology. That is the revolution in command and control—the ability to effect extraordinary centralization of command through the seemingly infinite capability of automatic data processing and modern communications, combined with the mobility of the helicopter. Fundamental change in the concept and practice of the chain of command appears certain; yet the concept of the responsibilities and practice of command is the nervous system of the professional ethos. Change in command practices is feared, if not actively opposed.

Today's America presents the Army with a difficult but stimulating challenge—to maintain ground power capability while engaged in self-correction of a large, diverse organization in response to changing domestic values. We believe that the job can be done—but only if the Army is prepared to face up to some very hard internal issues. The most difficult issues, as we see them, are as follows.

PRESERVATION OF VALUES

One of the more mundane truisms today is acknowledgement that American society is changing at a rapid, if not accelerating, pace. Various descriptions of the change have been advanced, and the more adventurous of the theoreticians have attempted to chart the future: Daniel Bell's post-industrial state, Herman Kahn's sensate society, Zbigniew Brzezinski's technetronic age—the third revolution, Charles Reich's Consciousness III, and the accelerating change of Alvin Toffler's Future Shock.

Each attempts to chart the dimensions of major change underway in American society, including our sense of values.

Each work overwhelms with statistics of change, but is understandably vague about probable institutional responsibilities and relationships in the future. Perhaps the frankest admission of uncertainty comes from John Gardner who has reflected that "We're like a man driving eighty miles per hour in a fog that permits him to see only thirty feet ahead."

The potential impact of such rapid change may be more pronounced for the military than it is for the rest of society. It jars the conservative bias of the military profession and erodes the traditional isolation which has served to preserve the professional ethic. During such a period of change, the challenge to the Army is to modify its policies and procedures to accommodate change, while retaining that essence of order and discipline which enables a unit to succeed in battle. The Army has often met this challenge; but, in the past, change was effected behind the protective barrier of isolation. Samuel P. Huntington has noted that the military profession is "probably unique among significant social institutions in the United States in the extent to which it was created independent of American society."

Change in the past was accomplished at a relatively leisurely pace. The Army had ample time to adjust to the new values stimulated by the Industrial Revolution as it dropped from public view in the late nineteenth and early twentieth centuries.

Today, the military appears to be no longer permitted the luxury of such self-paced, isolated change. One effect of the "technetronic age" has been to place the Army squarely in the center of the arena of rapid change. The effects of these changes upon the Army's relationship with American society are manifested in numerous ways:

National concern for the rights of the individual has focused critical attention on the military justice system. Military justice has become a subject of critical public attention to the extent of restricting the authority of the commander.

The mass communications media have maintained an unblinking eye on military activities. Griping and grousing by disgruntled servicemen consequently have become nationally advertised dissent.

National concern for equal opportunity for minorities has encouraged creation of racial organizations within and existing apart from the military chain of command.

The scourge of drug abuse has tied the military unit inexorably closer to the local community. Drug abuse can be met only through the closest coordination of policy and activity between adjacent military and civilian communities.

The problem of the moment does not appear to be military isolation from the civilian community. It is precisely the reverse. Given the apparent tendency of man in the post-industrial state toward increased social involvement and concern, the danger to national security and the military profession is that the unique characteristics and capabilities of the profession may become eroded beyond repair by overimmersion in such a rapidly changing value system. The Army must seek ways to promote the gradual adjustment to new American post-industrial values which will retain good order and discipline.

Some suggest that the only way to maintain an Army in the future will be to deliberately blur its functional role in an array of increased general social-welfare responsibilities. Such sentiment reflects the implicit fear that an army which retains its traditional image and structure is not supportable in the post-industrial America. Adam Yarmolinsky argues that, if the Army is to survive, it must "assume a lower and more flexible posture." To Yarmolinsky such a posture would cause a desirable and necessary erosion of military values: "As the military character of the military establishment becomes less distinctive, absolutist perceptions may be replaced by more realistic ones. The military may come to be regarded as any other part of government."

Yet the military character of the Military Establishment is

precisely what has been found to be essential to develop the order and discipline necessary to successful performance in war. The preservation of these values must come from within the Army. We must accentuate rather than conceal the fundamental military purpose of the Army.

> *Guideline:* The most pressing threat to military capability is over-exposure to rapidly shifting societal values. Isolation to preserve identity is preferable to immersion to stimulate rapid accommodation.

PRIMACY OF COMBAT READINESS

The dominant and overriding criterion for the evaluation of all Army programs must be the contribution of that activity to the honest combat readiness of the Army. In these days and times there are numerous calls for other uses of Army resources. Some would have the Army engage in socially "meaningful" activities which would contribute to the alleviation of pressing social ills of the nation. The general proposition that such activities could assist in resolving pressing problems is perhaps true. It does not follow, however, that the Army, charged with national defense responsibilities, should engage in such activities at any detriment to combat readiness.

Many socially relevant activities are being undertaken today by the Army. Programs such as equal opportunity for minorities and drug rehabilitation are necessary contributors to the unit cohesiveness that is an essential element of readiness. Other tasks are being undertaken by support units where skills employed in domestic action are identical to those required in supporting combat operations such as road building and medical care. Further, the post commander has broad responsibilities as the "mayor" of his installation. He should be an "enlightened mayor" to better care for his soldiers and their families. There can be no objection to activities such as these, but they must be subordinate to unit readiness for the traditional combat role.

A second aspect of this issue is the range of responsibilities that the Army should pursue as a vehicle of national social change. There are two broad philosophical alternatives: First, the Army can respond to change gradually as it influences both society at large and our soldiers. The Army would respond, but as a follower. The alternative would be the Army as a vehicle to lead the nation in social change. In effect the nation would be capitalizing upon the Army as a disciplined social organization in order to advance change in areas such as upgrading the marginally productive or rehabilitating convicts. We believe that the Army should pursue the former path—an essentially passive role responsive to change but not innovating. Current shifts in values and aspirations of youth are sufficiently challenging to development of order and discipline without adding additional burdens. Some federal or local agency that does not have the responsibility to produce disciplined performance under fire can seek new horizons of social responsibility. If the Army loses its ability to perform in combat, it loses all.

> *Guideline:* The primary social responsibility of the Army is to defend the nation.

PROFESSIONAL INTEGRITY

Integrity becomes an elusive attribute in large organizations where interlocking jurisdictions can diffuse if not actively discourage acceptance of personal responsibility. The

natural impetus of large organizations is to create inter-
changeable "faceless bureaucrats" skilled in the art of
manipulating and compromising difficult issues. The institutional search for the security of uniformity becomes the
opiate of personal initiative and responsibility. This, added to
the increasing reliance on impersonal reports for management
of rewards and promotions, creates an extraordinary conservatism in most people. "Don't rock the boat" becomes the
leitmotif of organization.

If the Army never had to go to war, it could continue
along—inefficient perhaps, but satisfied as it conforms to an
organizationally circumscribed definition of competence.
However the Army did go to war eventually and insofar as it
complied with inappropriate peacetime practices, it served
the Nation and itself poorly. Each serviceman has seen
situations that were wrong, in varying degree. Very few in the
officer corps "stood up to be counted" on the inadequacies
of the overly detailed Army Training Test checklist in Europe
or on body count, base camp luxuries, or other legacies of
peacetime which followed to Vietnam—legacies of the
hypocrisy of "looking good" or the cheery "Can Do" as a
sign of alert readiness despite the hidden costs of troop time.
Even worse, many tolerated the quibbling of a reporting
system conditioned to tell the commander what he wanted to
hear.

The continuing challenge and the present opportunity is to
seize upon recent experience as the stimuli to purge the
Army of practices which erode the sense of personal
responsibility without sacrificing traditional military values.
The criterion for change cannot be "improvement" to
develop better management as measured by theorists in
business organization or by experts in the resource management field. The criterion must be the recreation of and the
preservation of management practices which reward individualism, personal honesty, and moral courage rather than
impose uniform compliance to the system. Our management

system must stimulate and reward personal integrity. In far too many cases, it fails to do so today.

> *Guideline:* Reorient management practices to emphasize individual acceptance of responsibility.

ACCEPTANCE OF DIVERSITY

The organizational search for uniformity has had a second detrimental effect on the Army. It has created a myth of the desirability of uniform policies and practices across the diverse needs of the Army. It seems self-evident that the airborne infantryman faces a far different world than does the sophisticated electronics repairman. Each has widely differing environments. Attempts to develop one life style satisfactory to attract and retain each as a volunteer may result in an unhappy compromise—an undisciplined infantryman and an unhappy technician each continually frustrated as he seeks greater technical competence. The Modern Volunteer Army concept may be just such an unhappy compromise.

Unfortunately, the least-common-denominator life style can be a source of alienation and frustration. Alienation develops from dissatisfaction with the dishonesty and pretense surrounding attempts to enforce one pattern of conduct. Frustration develops as the individual seeks the life style he wants. One man finds satisfaction in a highly structured, authoritarian environment of high traditional esprit and danger while another craves the satisfaction of vocational improvement leading to union journeyman status in a comfortable environment.

The Army should encourage such different motivations by establishing an institutional and professional framework for diversity. Institutionally, some form of pluralistic Army recognizing a "combat" force and a "support" force should be adopted. Policies for awarding proficiency pay in the past have recognized just such a distinction. It is time to verify the distinction with policies consistent with and contributory to the requirements of the combat and support elements of the Army. At the same time, we should develop broader concepts of professionalism to accommodate a more pluralistic officer corps.

> *Guideline:* Encourage a diverse, pluralistic Army consisting of a combat and a support army, and encourage development of a more pluralistic concept of professionalism.

EQUALITY OF TREATMENT

Equal opportunity is closely allied to diversity as a source of hypocrisy and pretense in the Army. The Army is not and cannot pretend to be based upon equality of responsibility of personnel. It is and shall remain an authoritarian organization with responsibilities and privileges allocated in accordance with each individual's job or Military Occupational Specialty (MOS) and his position in the hierarchy (rank). However, job and position should be based upon fair evaluation of the individual's level of performance. In many cases this has not been done. There have been far too many examples of acts of bias or prejudice committed amid protestations of impartiality.

Equality of treatment has other more controversial implications. First, in a volunteer environment, the Army needs as many competent soldiers as it can attract. Neither race nor sex should be restrictive characteristics. In other words, black, white, red, or yellow, male or female, we want the competent motivated individual who wants to join a quality Army. "Ms." as opposed to "Miss" or "Mrs." is not a relevant issue. To us the distinction must be rank and job. In principle, for example, discrimination against women should be based solely upon MOS or rank just as it should be for all other members of the Army. Current social mores, however, require gradual transition to equality for women. The average American may not yet be prepared to accept female combat casualties.

A second implication is equality of treatment before the law. Each individual should have formal and informal avenues for the resolution of grievances. The Uniform Code of Military Justice (UCMJ) must remain as a strong yet fair framework for justice. Supplementary mechanisms should be provided, however, as additional insurance that each individual receives impartial consideration of his grievances. Some form of improved Inspector General or an Ombudsman channel of complaint could be established. The intent of these measures would be in no way to erode the sources or practices of discipline in the Army. Rather, it is to reinforce the fabric of mutual respect and understanding which are essential to willing discipline and order by developing institutional incentives for commanders to live up to the rhetoric of equality.

> *Guideline:* Project policies of fair, just discrimination based upon rank or job, not race or sex.

UNITY OF AUTHORITY

In these days of expanding pressures to ensure preservation of individual rights, frequent reference is made to the need for some form of collective bargaining to protect soldiers

—unionization of the armed forces as policemen and firemen have been organized in some areas. We believe that this is an issue where there can be no compromise—there can be no unionization insofar as it implies any derogation of the authority of the commander. This does not imply that the Army should not do much more to improve the conditions of service .of its men. As indicated when discussing equality, much remains to be done. However, a fundamental premise of the Army is that the commander, who bears the ultimate responsibility in the affairs of men, life or death, must be given the maximum discretion to accomplish his mission with a minimum loss of life. The gravity of the stakes involved in the military profession demands a basic and fundamental presumption that the commander is deeply and irrevocably concerned about the welfare of his men. With soldiers' lives in the balance, the leader *must* be skilled, competent, and concerned. If he is not, he must be and he will be relieved. It must be an absolute standard in the face of the absolute finality of death.

No union can be expected to accept responsibilities of this magnitude. It comes only with the attributes of profession. Conversely, the Army cannot accept the presumption of fallibility of leadership implicit in unionization and continue to retain its ethos as a profession.

Guideline: There can be no dissolution of the authority of the commander by unionization or formation of other subgroupings.

AVOIDANCE OF INDIVIDUAL UNDEREMPLOYMENT

"The basic challenge and attraction of service in the Army is the enormous satisfaction of serving with other young

Americans in well-equipped units assigned relevant missions and then left alone to get the job done" (Chief of Staff, "Building a Better Army," TV Script, 1971).

A basic assumption underlying this statement is the premise that our men are gainfully occupied—that they are engaged in useful work for an understandable purpose over a definable period. Unfortunately the premise has been erroneous more often than it has been true. Soldiers have been subject to "hurry up and wait" or "busy work" frequently in the past. Such misuse of personnel has been endemic in under-resourced or poorly led units. It can no longer be tolerated. Such use of manpower is wasteful of a limited and costly resource in a volunteer Army, and more seriously, such inactivity erodes the sense of job satisfaction which must exist if soldiers are to remain in the Army. Today's soldier must be occupied performing tasks relatable to his combat responsibilities—training or maintenance of person, equipment, or habitation—or he should be free to occupy himself as he wishes.

Few tasks are more difficult to implement in a large organization for it implies the decentralization of major questions of time allocation to small units. Further, it assumes local commanders possess sufficient moral courage to stand up and admit that the task has been completed early or that the job didn't really require the level of resources provided. General institutional guidance is required to encourage more realistic use of the soldier's time. It may be useful to encourage local commanders to develop guidance for the allocation of unit time. For example, guidance that maintenance of combat readiness for a certain type unit at a specified level of training and rate of personnel turnover could require three days of demanding day and night training, one day of maintenance, one day for personal improvement of the soldier, and two days of free time for the soldiers. We have much to do to encourage more realistic and honest allocation of soldiers' time.

Guideline: Encourage guidance relating maintenance of unit readiness levels to various allocations of unit personnel and time.

EMPHASIS ON THE FIELD ENVIRONMENT

The Army should never have to be reminded to insist on field training; the instinct to train should be basic. Unfortunately, intense competition for resources has tended to focus attention on more consistently measurable aspects of unit readiness such as combat vehicle or weapons characteristics, equipment deadline rates, or weapons qualification scores. Readiness which is achievable only by extensive and expensive field operations is truly measurable only by the ultimate test of conflict. In face of the infrequency of such testing, resources flow to the quantifiable—the hard data which can be assimilated by management information systems, the data which become measurable quantifiers of success relative to one's peers.

Understandable as it may be, any reduction in field training is doubly regrettable. It reduces actual combat readiness and with it the sense of inner confidence and satisfaction which reward the long hours and hard work. More critically, prolonged absence from field training exacerbates morale and discipline stresses within units. A key to resolution of complex social problems such as racial stress is the demonstration of authority and competence in the field environment. The delineation of officer-NCO responsibilities becomes clearly understandable only in the field. Garrison issues such as length and style of hair become minor as the chain of command can develop other, more credible "combat relatable" vehicles for demonstration of the utility and legitimacy of authority.

Guideline: Increase resources devoted to improved field training.

MAINTENANCE OF TRADITIONAL
LEADERSHIP AND DISCIPLINE

In recent years the Army has been confronted with a set of new conditions which have caused it to re-examine traditional leadership practices. Genuine and necessary concern over manifestations of minority group consciousness, potential racial disturbances, drug abuse, and a more questioning attitude on the part of young people in general has prompted the search for new patterns of relationships between leaders and led. This concern has been healthy and motivated by dedication to the highest interests of the service. Certainly it has revealed the inadequacy of many practices which have outlived their usefulness. But we believe that it is essential that this search not obscure the primacy of discipline as the foundation of the military. Discipline—the acceptance of authority—is the key not only to combat effectiveness, but to achieving harmonious relationships within the ranks and in limiting self-destructive and anti-social behavior such as drug abuse.

Soldiers, like all others within an ordered system, inherently feel for the limits of their freedom and understandably arrogate whatever slack there is in the system to their own advantage. If there is too much slack, order and harmony is destroyed by competing interests and life styles.

Soldiers must be conditioned to accept authority as a matter of routine. When this occurs, authority can wear a benign face. But that they do accept it is necessary. Developing an atmosphere in which authority is accepted and respected requires that the soldier subordinate himself to authority across a range of things which make up his daily life. How he wears his uniform, how he cuts his hair, saluting, and promptness are but a few of these. Enforcement of uniformly high standards for everyone without exception in such seemingly minor areas tends to have a carryover effect into other areas. The soldier who has accepted discipline in how he cleans his barracks has made a giant step toward becoming effective in his mission. Training or combat will be easier for him. He will approach them with an attitude of acceptance. We cannot wait until lives are in jeopardy to determine if soldiers do subordinate themselves to authority or to attempt to instill it at that point. Men must go into battle *already* disciplined. Failure to enforce high standards in little things creates an atmosphere of permissiveness. This fosters conditions within a military unit in which personal animosities, anti-social behavior, and racial polarization can flourish. It forces on the individual soldier a situation in which the limits of his acceptable behavior and of others is fuzzy and ill-defined. Usually he ends up with less freedom under such conditions than in one in which everybody knows the rules and has to follow them.

High standards are not justified merely for the sake of keeping order. Army units do not exist to provide employment or maintain static well-ordered communities of young people. They exist to provide combat power available to our government. Discipline, the acceptance of authority, is directly relevant to that purpose and must be so explained and justified.

This is a basic premise which has guided effective fighting forces throughout history. Discipline is essential. Commanders and leaders must have the authority to enforce it where necessary—regardless of what groups of soldiers may do to challenge authority or fail to meet high standards. Intelligent leaders will not abuse this authority, but without it they cannot produce combat capability. There is nothing particularly new or exotic about leading young Americans today. Time-honored practices—the maintenance of standards, knowing yourself, your men and your job are as relevant today as they were centuries ago. What is new is the complex management structure within which leadership and discipline is expected to develop. It is a management structure which seeks consensus—a system which seeks to avoid hard abrasive differences of view. It is a system which can breed self or superior-oriented conformists, a system oriented to perform for the quantifiable present rather than prepare for the immeasurable future. The institution must be modified to stimulate and reward sharp confrontations of opposing views up to the point of decision.

A second factor eroding leadership and discipline is derived from genuine difficulties in managing a large, extensive, disparate Army operating worldwide. Improved communications and information-processing techniques have been developed to provide extraordinary centralization of control of assets. They have permitted the development of complex, sophisticated, and highly competent mechanisms for ensuring efficient allocation of resources. Such sophistication has been introduced in the Army by the managerial bent of civilian authority applying the techniques of service in large civilian organizations and by the information demands of increasingly informed reviews conducted by Congress. These pressures have created a subtle but strong search for efficiency, a search which has often resulted in the unit in the field being used to demonstrate the prowess of the Army in using resources in order to justify more resources. Over time, the field unit has become the malleable resource shaped to serve Washington.

This emphasis is fundamentally wrong. The headquarters of the Army exists to support the units in the field, to make the tasks of the local commander from theater level to platoon leader less difficult. Efficiency is necessary; however, the ultimate criterion for evaluation of success is not efficient allocation of resources. Perhaps *reductio ad absurdum,* war is the ultimate uneconomic use of resources. The criterion of success must be actual employment of resources in the field environment with tired, average American soldiers trying hard but committing human errors. The evaluator of success is the intuitive judgment of the senior commander during peacetime; it is victory or defeat in wartime.

The key to leadership and discipline is recognition by Army management of the basic, essentially irrational, intuitively untidy need to decentralize asset control to local commanders. The Army must tolerate if not stimulate local solutions to local problems; it must have the moral courage to become "inefficient." It must remain human if it is to attract the hardy individualists who are the strength of America and who provide the leadership and discipline which has served the nation so well over the years. Only then can the balance between the managerial efficiency and the combat effectiveness of the Army be restored.

> *Guideline:* Decentralize to re-establish the primacy of the tactical unit.

It should be evident from the breadth of the guidelines we have proposed that we envisage rejuvenation of the basic values which have guided the Army so well in the past. We believe that some Army policies and practices which were perfectly acceptable for the internal imperatives and external threats of industrial America are no longer relevant to the challenges of coalition security and post-industrial America. Three issues appear to us to best highlight the range of necessary change. They are acceptance of institutional and professional diversity, primacy of combat readiness, and professional integrity. We shall elaborate on each of these issues in the following chapters.

Chapter 11

A PLURALISTIC ARMY

The diverse forces acting in post-industrial America combined with the new technological complexities of readiness for national defense make it increasingly difficult to maintain uniform policies and practices across the wide range of Army units and skills. To begin with, fewer and fewer of our men in uniform today are actually engaged in duties directly related to combat—that is, who possess the occupational specialty of infantryman, artilleryman, or armored crewman—and greater numbers of soldiers and officers are assigned duties relating to support rather than combat. Although some critics of the Army in Congress and elsewhere have deplored this trend, it is in fact no more than the military reflection of the generalized trend of employment evident in all modern societies, as manifested, for example, in the greater numbers of persons found in the secondary and tertiary sectors of society rather than the primary industries. The decreasing

AUTHORS' NOTE: In preparing this chapter we are indebted to the counsel of Anthony A. Smith, who, in disagreement, sharpened our focus on the issues of a pluralistic Army. Also, in our analysis of the model pluralistic Army we are indebted to the stimulating work accomplished recently by Charles Moskos, "The Emergent Military: Civilianized, Traditional or Pluralistic?" (A paper presented at the 1971 annual meeting of the American Political Science Association.)

combat-to-support ratio—or "teeth-to-tail" ratio, as some have termed it—is not only natural but also has some desirable effects. For one thing, it has resulted in the diminution of casualty and death rates in each successive war in which America has become involved—surely a laudable achievement.

At the same time as the relative size of the combat portion of the Army has decreased, however, there is an increasing dichotomy between the role of the combat soldier and the support soldier. For the soldier engaged in combat, "soldiering" has changed little over the years. To be sure, he has a better weapon to fire and a more modern mode of transportation, but his basic function of seeking the enemy on the ground in order to defeat him remains unchanged. Such a role leads inexorably, just as it did in Napoleon's day, to physical hardship, unpleasant living conditions, and danger to life. And such a role also dictates the need for the same soldierly attributes and discipline which have been demanded of the soldier over the years.

The support soldier, on the other hand, finds little resemblance between his job and function and the soldiering of yesteryear. For him, being a soldier may mean that he is first and foremost a mechanic, or a radar technician, or a computer programmer practicing a trade which differs little, if at all, from that practiced by his civilian counterparts. It follows, of course, that the support soldier will likely find more in common with persons outside the military establishment who have similar jobs than with the combat soldiers, with whom they may have little shared experience other than the uniform they both wear.

We feel that the single approach taken by the Army today as it seeks to maintain uniform policies and practices across the wide range of Army units and skills is becoming increasingly difficult to maintain. Such a uniform traditional approach cannot accommodate the sort of life style which the support soldier will find appealing. On the other hand, more liberal attitudes such as those advocated by the Modern Volunteer Army concept threaten to erode the discipline essential to the combat Army. We see no uniform range of policies which can span these differences, for combat soldiers will continue to be attracted by the psychic stimulant of performance in the face of personal danger. Yet what stimulates the infantryman may be an anathema to the radar technician, who is primarily motivated to enter the service by the opportunity to learn a civilian-related skill. This is a difference of perspective which cannot be bridged by uniform policies.

The purpose of this chapter is to suggest several policies which could be undertaken by the Army to adjust to the requirements of a pluralistic Army which will attract and retain quality manpower in competition with the American economy, while adjusting to pressure for diversity.

The design of a pluralistic Army must be influenced by several basic considerations. First and foremost, we must maintain an open mind. As noted above, there is increasing divergence between the values and aspirations of those whom we would desire to recruit for the combat skills (some 25% of total accessions) and those who would perform support skills not greatly dissimilar from civilian life. The trend of Army policy, particularly as the Army progresses to an all-volunteer force, has been to attempt to bridge the gap between these increasingly divergent skills and motivations by finding a middle ground of standards. As the gap broadens, however, compromise may present the Army with infantrymen too undisciplined to fight and technicians frustrated to the point of resignation by overly authoritarian discipline. Thus, we believe that the Army must seriously evaluate the true merits and costs of attempting to maintain "one Army" standards. A pluralistic Army should not be rejected based on the emotion of outdated tradition.

Second, the Army is not intended to be a cauldron of social change. Our responsibility is to defend the country, responding as required to social changes in the body politic. When we advocate increased reliance on women, for example, we do so from the standpoint of attracting the number of skills required to maintain ground-power capability commensurate with potential national requirements. We believe that use of the talents of women is necessary to achievement of this goal. Women are capable of performing most of the skills required in the Army. We need them if we are to maintain necessary defense readiness in a volunteer environment.

Third, the Army must not lose one of its unique basic strengths—the ability to respond well in completely unforeseen contingencies. The Army has traditionally possessed the management talents and leadership necessary at critical moments in the history of our nation. To provide but a few examples, the Army played the central role in developing the West. At a time of national crisis brought about by the economic depression of the 1930s, the nation turned to the Army to organize and run the Civilian Conservation Corps. When called upon in Vietnam, it provided many of the skilled public servants required to man the AID, USIA, and CIA efforts. The Army is unique as an agency of government. It is the most flexible, competent organization for managing complex unanticipated national programs. This is a unique strength. The pluralistic Army must preserve if not enhance this capability.

Lastly and most importantly, the Army must at all times retain the ability to fight. Changes must not be permitted to result in any diminution of land power capability at least as effective as the status quo.

THE MODEL

To elaborate how a more pluralistic Army might eventually develop, we have described a model below. We hold no particular brief for the specifics of the recommendations herein which are intended primarily to illustrate the concept. We believe that it is useful to portray an alternative basis of organization as a vehicle for discussion. It is not intended as a blueprint for a wholesale retransformation of the Army, but rather as a technique for exploring various issues within a coherent and consistent conceptual framework. It is important to realize that if indeed greater diversification and pluralism is developed, this would have important implications throughout the structure. It seems to us that this "fleshing out" of the concept in various particulars is in fact a necessary basis for making judgments concerning the desirability of various, perhaps seemingly unrelated policy changes under consideration. Where are we trying to go? What are the tendencies of our actions? If something approximating the model we describe is considered desirable and appropriate, then certain policy initiatives in various areas would appear desirable also—OPMS being a case in point (see Chapter 12 on officer career patterns). Of course the reverse is equally true. If the paradigm suggested is not the kind of Army believed necessary, then changes tending in that direction would be considered counter to long-term objectives.

A pluralistic Army would consist of two broad sub-groupings of skills—a combat Army composed of those individuals and organizations primarily designed to close with and destroy the enemy (combat and combat-support units) and a support Army composed of those personnel and organizations required to support a modern ground force (combat service support units). A comparison of possible policies in key areas for the enlisted and non-commissioned

Army is as follows: Chapter 13 addresses the impact of a
Pluralistic Army on the officer corps.

Organization

The combat Army would consist of the traditional combat
arms (infantry, armor, and artillery) plus those combat and
service units normally employed within the combat area of
operations. Reserve units would orient to the combat or
support responsibilities which the unit would assume when
called to active service. A rough division by arm or service
could be:

> *Combat Army:* Infantry, Armor, Field Artillery, Air Defense
> Artillery as well as Engineer, Signal Corps, Military Intelligence,
> and Military Police units normally employed within the division.
> Units training personnel for combat service would be considered
> to be within the combat army.

> *Support Army:* Support services such as: Adjutant General Corps,
> Finance, Transportation, Ordnance, Quartermaster, and the pro-
> fessional services (medical and legal) employed to the rear of the
> division operational area.

Ethos

The combat Army would pursue the traditional professional ethos—service to country with unlimited liability to,
and including the risk of, death. The expectation of service
would be challenging, personally dangerous service to the
nation performed in a difficult, intensely physical environment. The support Army would subject soldiers to personal
danger only under unusual circumstances. The basic satisfaction of service in the support Army would be the
satisfaction of technical competence in complex civilian-
related skills.

Service Incentives

Service in the combat Army would be rewarded by incentives designed to compensate for the inherent risks as well as the lack of opportunity to develop civilian-related skill for a second career. Combat soldiers would thus be offered such incentives as a combat Army enlistment bonus, expanded "second career" vocational training upon retirement (an extended GI Bill for combat soldiers), and accelerated retirement benefits (double time in the combat Army for retirement purposes, e.g., five years service in the combat Army would provide the same retirement benefits as ten years service in the support Army).

The support Army would reward service by increased competence in civilian-related skills. Close affiliation would be maintained with civilian unions. Lateral entry at NCO level would be encouraged. Improved technical specialization would be stimulated by permitting frequent "sabbaticals" with civilian industry. The support soldier would receive additional training periodically to ensure that his level of technical competence improves throughout his service at a rate comparable to that of his civilian contemporaries.

Promotion policy would favor the combat soldier both as an incentive to service and due to the physical demands of leadership of combat forces. Combat Army leaders would face accelerated promotion and force out—E-7 at 25 to 30, E-8 at 30 to 35, and E-9 at 40 years age. The support Army would have very liberal promotion policies permitting relatively low specialist grades at age 40 to 45. Highly qualified master specialists would be permitted to remain on active service until age 60. More rapid promotion would be possible but exceptional. The attraction of service in the support Army is the satisfaction of public service through continued improvement in technical competence in a stable, financially secure environment.

Discipline

Discipline in the combat Army would stress traditional authoritarian patterns. The fabric of leadership would continue to be mutual respect based upon demonstrated professional competence and respect for the aspirations and limitations of each individual soldier. Leadership would remain understanding and tolerant but clearly and unequivocally based upon strict obedience to lawful orders of higher authority. There is room and necessity for great variation in styles to permit the appropriate response to diverse leadership challenges; however, variations would be expected to reinforce, not vitiate, the basic order and discipline essential in a combat unit.

The support Army would place greater emphasis than the combat Army on the more conventional industrial-management techniques of participatory leadership and the development of group consensus. Aside from certain minimum standards of dress, appearance, and conduct which would remain uniform throughout the Army, the standards of required performance would be those prescribed by the requirements of successful performance in the particular support skill.

Grievance satisfaction procedures would parallel those developed for the maintenance of discipline. The combat soldier would be served by the traditional Inspector General system augmented by some form of ombudsman relationship within tactical units. The support Army would rely on the establishment of craft associations operating subordinate to commanders of large units—support brigades and higher. Direct relationships would be encouraged with skill-related civilian organizations to encourage individual development to higher skill levels. As discussed in Chapter 10, there could be no derogation of the authority of the unit commander.

Equal Opportunity

The combat Army would practice full equal opportunity irrespective of race or background. For the foreseeable future, however, no women would be included since public opinion would be reluctant to support such an innovation. Equal opportunity would be facilitated by expanded educational or training programs for the less skilled. Such training provided at the basic training center would be designed to ensure approximately equal soldier ability upon assignment to his tactical unit. Once in the unit, rewards such as promotion would be allocated on a rough quota basis to ensure that there is fair and equal recognition of minority groups within units. In short, racial .tolerance is highly desirable and should be stimulated by unit educational programs but such change is complex to achieve. In fact, it may be generational in nature. For the short term, we must be prepared to "legislate morality" by establishing specific decision rules to enforce equal opportunity.

Similar practices should be pursued in the support Army with one addition—no discrimination based upon sex. We believe that the support Army must accept women in all MOS for which they are physically qualified. The Women's Army Corps (WAC) would exist only to conduct basic Army training of women. Advanced individual training (Combat Support Training) for females across the full range of support skills would be completely integrated with training for males. The only assignment limitation for females would concern housing—there must be female barracks or the opportunity to live in private accommodations off-post.

Several measures would be required to ensure true equal opportunity between males and females. Promotion quotas (officer and NCO) would be established to ensure that women are promoted along with their male competitors. These "slices" should extend to the general officer ranks within the support Army. Similar controls would be applied across all morale and discipline indicators to ensure fair and equal treatment irrespective of race, background, or sex in the support Army.

Some may misunderstand what we mean by equal opportunity in the support Army. We would foresee such situations as a signal maintenance company commanded by white female captain with a black male executive officer and a white male first sergeant, working for a black female general support maintenance battalion commander in a support brigade commanded by a white male colonel as one major subordinate element in a logistics command commanded by a black female general officer (logistics). The choice of race and sex in the preceding example is, of course, only illustrative. The point is that with fully equal opportunity and suitable time for implementation, the support Army should consist of females and minority groups spread throughout the grade structure in proportions similar to those in the civilian work force. There would be similar distribution in staff assignments to and including the Headquarters, Department of the Army.

One caveat is necessary. Equal opportunity should in no manner vitiate the healthy competition essential to a dynamic innovative organization. Minority groups and females must be prepared to be dismissed or reduced on a fully comparable basis with white males. The Army is not an instrument of social reform to correct past injustice. Rather, the Army needs and expects the best talents available in the entire national manpower pool irrespective of race or sex. The competitive process must be fair and impartial within the unit. Promotion or assignment quotas would be necessary to ensure compliance across the Army at large but they should be administered locally with great discretion. Elimination quotas should be handled with similar discretion. Properly used, they should be equally representative of race and sex and should counterbalance any race or sex bias which might be perceived in the promotion flow.

Education and Training

The base structure of education and training within the combat Army would change little. The combat arms employment schools, the current structure of individual and unit training, and the three-tiered NCO education system presently being established would all be continued with normal and necessary modifications to reflect improved knowledge of the educational process.

The support Army would rely heavily on civilian industry. Technical service schools and an Administrative/Logistics Technical College suitable for advanced instruction in the military application of technical skills should provide sufficient professional content. These should be complemented with use of civilian skill improvement centers for NCOs. NCOs would expect continuing upgrading of their technical skills throughout their term of service.

Common Policies

The comparison above focuses on differences, each designed to correspond to the disparate needs of the Army and to the differing aspirations of the possessors of particular skills. But the Army, if it is to remain a viable dynamic organization, must balance its tolerance of diversity with the institution of unifying influences to reinforce the soldier's sense of identity with the larger organization. In a number of key areas, such as the unified justice system which is provided by the Uniform Code of Military Justice, policies would remain identical to those presently pursued. In certain aspects they would be extended to reinforce a single Army identity. Areas of standard, unifying policy would be:

Base standards of personal appearance: Uniform and other aspects of personal appearance would be similar throughout the entire Army. Different accessories such as badges or berets are desirable to enhance unit distinctiveness but there would be one uniform, absolute standard of appearance. We believe that the Army should expect its members to demonstrate publicly subordination of individual whim to central discipline by adopting relatively conservative standards of personal appearance and uniform for *all* serving members. The Army should accept the symbology of the uniform and exploit it as a useful symbol of basic general acceptance of authority. Maintenance of one standard of personal appearance and uniform represents the common identity and the acceptance of minimum standards of discipline expected of any member of the Army. All within the Army must be prepared to enforce this standard.

Heritage: Some form of regimental system should be developed to stress the tradition and esprit of the Army. Unit uniform accessories stressing regimental heritage should be encouraged. Other measures would include repetitive assignments within a regiment and regimental home basing and recruiting. Further, support Army units would be associated with combat Army regiments and be encouraged to capitalize on the support relationship. These are only representative proposals. The point is that the Army has great traditions and heritage which should be exploited as a unifying force. At present we seem deliberately to subordinate individual unit identity and pride to standardization on the image of the basic infantryman. The increased complexity of war and diversity of individual motivation for military service call into serious question the continuing validity of this assumption.

Basic Training: All soldiers (eventually perhaps to include some women) would take combat arms basic training. Any soldier could find himself in a combat situation and should therefore receive a basic exposure to combat Army skills. Further, all soldiers should have an understanding of the role and problems of the basic combat infantryman—the heart of ground power.

Life style: Facilities would be provided to soldiers and

their families irrespective of membership in the combat or support Army. Army Community Services, housing, dependents schooling, and other support facilities would be identical throughout the Army. Hopefully there would be general improvement in the overall quality of such services as the Army continues to accept increased responsibility for the total environment of its soldiers. As products of our affluent society, young Americans expect that a profession should provide for their wives, cars, and pets. The Modern Volunteer Army concept has directed resources to general life style improvements. Further, redisposing the NATO force would call for new, more comprehensive acceptance of responsibility for Army families. These efforts should continue as a unifying influence within an increasingly diverse profession.

As a large, diverse organization with continuing national defense responsibilities, the Army will always be reluctant to institute such basic and far-reaching change such as we propose. Such reluctance is justified and based on natural conservatism combined with genuine concern about potential change in the traditionally satisfactory relationship between the Army and our democratic society. For example, despite the many areas of unifying policies, some will be concerned that there is implicit danger that division of the Army may provoke unwanted change in the characteristics of either of the component parts. The support Army with increased separation from the combat Army could become less responsive to the 24-hours-per-day 7-days-per-week requirements of national defense. In short, the fear would be that the support Army, increasingly proficient in civilian-related skills, would adopt the hours and perspectives of civilian interest groups. Eventually, this perspective could be reinforced if the support Army were to engage in a wide range of socially productive tasks for the nation at large through domestic employment of its support skills. We do not believe that such concern should impede more active social roles, however, for they would improve the basic readiness of the support Army to perform its wartime mission. Aware of such separatist sentiment, the Army should emphasize "one Army" similarities and conduct frequent training exercises reflecting the interdependence of combat and support armies.

As some become concerned about the erosion of values in the support Army, others may foresee an isolated self-serving "praetorianism" developing in the combat Army. This does not seem to us to be a valid danger. As was discussed in the preceding chapters, all parts of the Army stand squarely in the center of the arena of rapid social change. For example, race and drug problems tie the combat commander inexorably to the local community. Furthermore, the combat Army will be separated from the support Army only during the rare occasions when there is active combat. The normal ready posture of both combat and support armies will be co-location on large posts. Thus, the whole range of social intercourse will serve to tie the two forces together.

Some of the characteristics described for the pluralistic Army such as variable retirement benefits and variable promotion rates would require Congressional authorization. They would also require time and considerable debate to implement. That is good—the far-reaching nature of several of the proposals is such that they would have to be explained carefully to the Army at large and then implemented over a decade or more. The crucial element, however, is not the rapidity of transition to new policies. Rather, it is the general recognition that simply "muddling through" may not provide the Army that the nation expects and deserves. Basic change in Army policy as it has existed for nearly two hundred years is required if the Army is to continue as a vibrant innovative national defense force. This is the basic issue of the pluralistic Army. Is the Army prepared to adjust in order to accommodate the diversity that is America today?

Chapter 12

THE SOCIAL RESPONSIBILITIES OF THE ARMY

Second only to the challenge of diversity is the issue of the basic responsibility of the Army to our democratic society. The assertion has been made, within the professional ranks, that the Army must become "meaningful" if it is to continue to exist. The proposition is most often stated to buttress arguments favoring the development of non-combat-related "socially productive" roles which will not only keep the Army active and committed to the mainstream of American life, but also, because of their utility to the nation, will serve as added justification for the continued existence of the Army.

We believe that this proposition is wrong. The greatest current danger to the Army is the stimulus to over-involvement in efforts to maintain social "relevance" rather than any isolation stimulated by under-involvement. The evolving nature of the American society constitutes a reasonable guarantee that the problem for the military profession is not lack of social integration; the character of our post-industrial society will insure that the necessary ties continue to be maintained, even in an all-volunteer force. The Army is already deeply committed to a broad range of social welfare programs. Further, there has been a trend of continually increasing involvement. Isolation is not the problem.

The real challenge to the Army today is to conduct responsible and necessary social welfare programs, while preserving the order and discipline which combine to produce combat units who willingly serve the national defense with "unlimited liability"—to and including the ultimate price. The danger is over-commitment to social welfare programs which can erode the basic readiness to fight which is the lifeblood of the Army. The concern is not that the Army exercises social responsibilities. Many are absolutely necessary for management of the armed forces or to perform an essential public service such as disaster assistance or civil defense planning. The problem is to responsibly subordinate acceptance of social welfare programs to adequate defense readiness.

We are not starting with a blank slate. The Army is engaged today in a broad series of social programs developed over the years in response to general acceptance of an increasing governmental role in providing for the social welfare of individuals and in taking direct responsibility for many other important areas of public life. Current social programs in which the Army is involved have historical precedent in a general tradition of civic assistance provided over the years by the Army.

However, in the past the Army neither saw itself, nor was it seen by others, as possessing enduring responsibilities to conduct programs to improve the lot of any particular individuals in society or to correct social ills which plague the nation. Since World War II there has been increasing pressure to commit the Army to social programs involving improvement of the individual. Some programs were necessary for better management of the armed forces; others were intended to improve community relations by providing useful public services.

The rhetoric of leadership has led to the development of a broad set of social welfare programs, most of which are desirable for improvement of personnel management. Yet some programs directly affect the environment and life style of the individual citizen both in and out of military service. Major current efforts are: Domestic Action, Equal Opportunity (minority relations), General Education Development (education), Alcohol and Drug Abuse Prevention and Control, Project One Hundred Thousand, and Project Transition.

Domestic Action: This is a recent Department of Defense (DOD) "carrier" program for most externally oriented social welfare activities conducted by the military services under the guidance of a DOD Domestic Action Council. The program includes manpower efforts such as Project Referral, intended to assist in securing jobs for retirees; Project Value, designed to provide jobs in DOD for over 1,000 hard-core unemployed per year; and the Youth Employment Program, an effort to provide summer jobs for over 40,000 youths per year.

Military procurement is also channeled to minority small business enterprises. Physical resources (equipment, facilities, services, and property) are made available on a reimbursable basis where possible. Over 275,000 disadvantaged youth were provided recreational, cultural, educational, and training activities during the summer of 1969 in the community relations effort. Lastly, technical knowledge such as low-cost modular housing, aeromedical evacuation, and environmental improvement is provided to civilian communities. The sixth element of the program is equal rights which continues longstanding efforts in minority relations.

Equal Opportunity: Beginning with desegregation in 1948, the services have led the national effort in minority relations. Secretary Robert S. McNamara saw the services as "a powerful fulcrum in removing the barriers to racial justice not merely in the military, but in the country at large." Consistent with this philosophy, the DOD open housing policy predated the comparable provisions of the Civil Rights Act of 1968. In further extension of this activist social role, places of local entertainment practicing segregation have been placed off limits by the Secretary of the Army. Formal education in minority relations is being expanded for all service personnel. The level of involvement has increased each year.

General Education Development: The military is the largest vocational training institution in the United States. The rate of· turnover of personnel—an estimated 24,000,000 veterans since 1940—and the physical plant required have resulted in a major and expanding national educational system within the services.

Prior to Vietnam, approximately 500,000 individuals left the military services annually for civilian life with an estimated fifty per cent having received post-high school occupational and professional education and training. Such Army programs continue to increase dramatically. A $22,600,000 program in 1968 to increase high school, college, and post-graduate qualifications of all enlisted and officer grades may expand to over $40,000,000 for 1973.

More recently, the Modern Volunteer Army Program envisaged "an educational system which provides each soldier the opportunity to acquire, on duty time, civilian-recognized skills or education" so that the soldiers will see the Army "as an avenue and not as an alternative, to their personal and educational development." A policy of providing veteran benefits to insure that an individual did not suffer as a result of government service has become a program of providing personal benefit through government aid and assistance while serving and during duty hours—a new horizon of social responsibility for the Army.

Alcohol and Drug Abuse Prevention and Control: Although too early to gauge the long-term resource implications of this new program, the principal is clear. The military services are expected to provide professional rehabilitation for individuals discovered to be suffering from addiction during their period of national service. As is the case with educational programs, national service will, through rehabilitation, benefit the individual whether he acquired the disorder before or during service.

The drug abuse program will require over $38,000,000 of direct costs for fiscal 1973. Unsupported estimates of true cost to include salaries of addicts, guards for facilities, and so forth range up to $100,000,000 per year for the Army. All that seems certain at this point is that the military has entered into a new and uncharted area of social responsibility.

Project One Hundred Thousand: This project was developed by Secretary McNamara to broaden the manpower base and to make the marginally productive civilian into a successful, competitive citizen. He saw the challenge as:

> a ghetto of the spirit. Chronic failures in school throughout their childhood, they were destined to a sense of defeat and decay in a skill-oriented nation that requires from its manpower pool an increasing index of competence, discipline and self-confidence. Many of these men, we decided, could be saved.

From October 1, 1966, to September 30, 1971, the Army accepted over 200,000 of these individuals at an estimated annual cost for fiscal 1970 of under $3,000,000.

Project Transition: The objective of Project Transition has been to assist the soldier to secure a job upon completion of service. Begun in 1968, the program consists of job counseling, vocational training, and job placement assistance. By 1970, 240,000 men had been counseled, and 69,000 trained at 55 installations in the United States. Project Transition was expanded owing to the high veteran unemployment problem in the immediate aftermath of Vietnam.

Broad guidance is evident in the varying objectives, techniques, and beneficiaries of these six programs. The range of variation is so broad as to preclude establishment of unequivocal general criteria for evaluation of the suitability of programs. Of these programs, two—Minority Relations and Drug Abuse—address problems which directly affect the military readiness of units, as well as being programs which demonstrate acceptance of federal responsibility to state and local governments. Two other programs—General Education Development and Project One Hundred Thousand—improve individual skills for both service and post-service activity. A third, Project Transition, addresses only veteran activity.

Several of the Domestic Action and technical knowledge programs would cost very little and could make useful and necessary contributions to the improvement of life in the United States. Examples would be use of military posts as test vehicles for the development of new techniques of low-cost housing construction, mass transit systems, or pollution abatement. Other programs merely serve to open military resources to ghetto or rural poor much as service children have been accommodated in the past—for example, scouting and club activities. Some programs such as disaster relief are purely humanitarian. In the face of such diversity, program objective seems an inadequate criterion. Nor do any other external criteria appear more useful for the evaluation of the suitability of social programs. The criterion, therefore, must be internally oriented. That is, what is the impact of a particular social welfare program on combat readiness? Application of the combat readiness criterion is influenced by several general considerations. These considerations include Congressional and public perceptions of the role of an Army, the administrative difficulties involved in instituting complex social welfare programs, and the political impact of many social welfare programs.

It is a basic proposition that the Army exists to defend the nation. The Army must be skilled, tough, and ready to perform its mission in defending the country, and it must be seen as such by the American people who have a right to expect that several billion dollars per year will produce the necessary units with fully capable fighting troops. If such resources also produce some form of social benefit, so much the better, but the funds are appropriated to provide the basic military preparedness expected by Congress and the public.

Until recently, the Army has been assigned increased social welfare responsibilities during a period of increasing defense budgets. Today, the situation has changed; budgets have declined in real and absolute terms.

The major stimulus for allocation of national resources to the Army is, and must remain, basic Congressional acceptance of the need for a reasonable level of general defense readiness roughly divided to meet the land, sea, and air threats. It appears unlikely that social welfare projects could become a convincing rationale for allocation of additional military resources. More fundamentally, during periods of budgetary retrenchment, increased social welfare responsibilities could serve to dilute rather than create basic military readiness.

A second consideration is the difficulty of introducing complex social programs in large organizations. If a program is too complex or too innovative to be understood and honestly accepted by average men and women, it may fail despite the most optimistic prognostications of central authority. Racial-attitude conditioning, out-patient drug rehabilitation, and establishment of the environment of discipline based upon mutual trust called for by the Modern Volunteer Army Program are current attempts to institutionalize sophisticated social programs which strain the limits of current social knowledge, but which essentially are problems that local military commanders have been forced to solve. It is not certain that these programs can be implemented by average Army managers.

Requirements for quality personnel, sheer size, and the bureaucratic nature of the Army combine to make social action programs difficult to run properly. The Army, as a bureaucracy, may be a blunt instrument incapable of institutionalizing the finesse required to deal with complex social problems at the federal level. This inability is not unique to the Army; it is characteristic of large organizations.

Furthermore, the local commander is the cutting edge, innovating at the local level social change which was proposed at the theoretical level. To the average American the innovator is not Secretary McNamara or Secretary Melvin R. Laird. It is the Army. Adam Yarmolinsky (1971: 353) has observed: "The establishment has assumed a certain responsibility for stimulating social change and has ceased to be contented solely with maintaining the status quo of the society it serves." He is correct—but the burden is not borne by the "establishment" which comes and goes from public service. It is borne by the average captain and sergeant in the Army year after year.

Another vexing but oft-forgotten aspect of domestic action is the problem of allocation of resources at the local level. While Army motives may be humanitarian and pure, the allocation of resources is a function of political power. Politics is the process of resolving conflicting values and wants. When the Army provides resources to any civilian community, it becomes enmeshed in political processes. It cannot escape a role of direct or indirect influence. For example, are resources to be distributed through Republicans or Democrats? The Army can be placed in a difficult, untenable position.

These considerations counsel caution as the Army evaluates increased social welfare responsibilities. They suggest that distinct levels of involvement may be appropriate, commensurate with the extent to which increased participation contributes or detracts from the internal criterion of combat readiness.

We believe this approach is of equal validity for today's Army or for one which acknowledges a more explicit division between combat and support forces as described in Chapter 11. In the latter, the distinctive characteristics of the two major components of the force—the combat Army and the support Army—would adopt the approach suitable to their own unique attributes and requirements.

Units in the combat Army should actively support programs which contribute to the tactical readiness, morale, good order, and discipline of units. Since their primary mission, ground combat, is not basically civilian related, the general level of involvement would be modest.

The support Army, on the other hand, would probably be involved in a number of projects which provide civilian-related services such as light construction, medical care, or improvement of communications. One could foresee both the use of support units in a limited assistance role and the provision of management talent (officer and NCO) to civilian agencies on social welfare sabbaticals. In either case, a socially activist role could serve to enhance readiness to perform the combat mission.

Reorganization of the National Guard into federally supported State Militias would create a massive infrastructure capable of undertaking extensive social welfare projects at the state and local level. Army participation would be indirect and supportive in that the Army could provide technical assistance and training to state agencies. It could, nevertheless, be a major Army program instituted at the headquarters rather than the troop level. The Army should be able to effect genuinely valuable assistance to the Militias without detracting from unit readiness.

Several actions or policy guidelines could serve to reinforce the conservative policy direction we advocate:

—To display the range and costs of involvement, aggregate, and publicize the current level of Army participation in social welfare programs. Where possible, include both dollar and personnel costs with particular reference to the impact on the tactical unit.

—Evaluate ongoing or proposed programs on the basis of their impact on the readiness for combat of all units.

—Programs which directly, substantially contribute to the tactical readiness, morale, good order, and discipline of combat, combat support, and combat-service support units should be encouraged and increased. Examples of programs which could be increased are those to reduce racial and drug abuse problems in all units, off-duty educational and training improvement programs for soldiers, and social infrastructure assistance to the civilian community such as aeromedical evacuation or engineer construction projects which are unequivocal, direct applications of wartime combat-service support skills.

—Programs which serve to reduce directly the combat readiness of units should be reduced to the essential minimum. Examples of such programs are Project Transition, which could be accomplished by the Veterans Administration after the individual is no longer expected to be militarily ready, and Project One Hundred Thousand, which could be replaced with nonmilitary pretraining before an individual is expected to be prepared to accept national defense responsibilities.

Decisions on personnel programs with uncertain impact upon unit readiness should be decentralized to the local commander with decision guidance to plan, budget, and conduct projects which he believes will contribute to improved unit readiness. Projects impacting on civilian communities would be encouraged after detailed coordination and approval by the local political, business, and labor leadership. Examples of projects for decentralized leadership could be Special Forces operations, social action-oriented adventure training, or community relations projects such as summer camps. Other, more extensive programs could be undertaken by the support Army if such a pluralistic Army is accepted or by the reserve establishment or any successor organization.

This guidance would permit continuation, if not expansion, of a wide range of current projects which are shown to be demonstrably neutral politically, useful socially, and not detrimental to unit readiness. The Army policy theme must be willing acceptance of socially useful tasks insofar as they contribute to the building of proud, capable units—as perceived by the local commander responsible for unit readiness.

Complex major programs centrally administered and publicized such as race training and drug rehabilitation must be aggressively supported; they genuinely increase unit readiness. Decentralization of other projects to the local commander who is directly and immediately responsible will continue the essential pre-eminence of traditional roles and responsibilities of the Army. At that level, maintenance of the capability to fight is an instinctive response.

Policies such as these would reflect necessary positive acceptance of responsibility to meet and solve challenging social issues, yet preserve the unique nature of the profession. These policies and programs would be strictly subordinated to maintenance of combat readiness. However unpopular or "reactionary" these policies might seem to be, the Army must persevere:

> Upon the soldiers, the defenders of order rests a heavy responsibility. The greatest service they can render is to remain true to themselves, to serve with silence and courage in the military way. If they abjure the military spirit, they destroy themselves first and their nation ultimately [Huntington, 1957: 466].

Part IV

THE MILITARY PROFESSION IN A NEW ERA

Chapter 13

A PLURALISTIC PROFESSION

The Need for New Concepts. In previous chapters we have touched upon several areas which have an impact upon the nature of the military profession and upon the basic philosophy which motivates and gives a sense of identity and purpose to the career commissioned and non-commissioned officers of the Army. Attention was first focused upon the Army in terms of forces—as a combat structure. We argued that a greater degree of specialization was required within the active structure to provide for greater flexibility and better use of high-cost manpower and equipment. A better balance between support and combat structure was suggested to improve readiness without mobilization. These changes would accelerate the importance of numerous non-combat specialists within the active ranks.

We then dealt with the Army as an institution adapting to change and proposed the concept of a pluralistic Army to accommodate the diversity which is required in the active force and which parallels much of society.

AUTHORS' NOTE: The discussion in the section concerning professional expertise is based in part on Z. B. Bradford and J. N. Murphy, "A new look at the military profession," Army (1969).

[217]

If they are to endure these new prospectives must be compatible with the concepts of professionalism with which the career personnel identify. At the present time, this is not the case. The traditional view is one of a substantially unitary professionalism subordinating nearly all functional activities, regardless of how vital to the organization, to a model of the combat leader—to the "manager of violence" as described by Samuel Huntington. While this ethic is essential to the combat elements of the force, it can inhibit appropriate development of new attitudes necessary for the Army to diversify and to accommodate change. In this chapter we will therefore question the theoretical underpinnings of the profession as they have generally been accepted and offer some alternate views. We will then examine policy initiatives which could translate a more pluralistic concept of professionalism into career patterns for the officer corps.

Professional Expertise

To deal with the military as a profession, we may start with the definition by Samuel P. Huntington in *The Soldier and the State*—perhaps the best known, most widely accepted, and certainly the most methodically developed conceptualization.

Huntington states that the military is a profession because it possesses three characteristics common to all generally acknowledged professions and essential to professional status: expertise, responsibility, and corporateness. For the unique expertise of the military, he adopts from Harold Lasswell the concept of "management of violence." This is distinct from mere application of violence, such as physically firing weapons, for this ability gives only technical competence or tradesman status. All activities conducted within the military establishment, Huntington says, are related to this unique expertise: management of violence. This peculiar expertise is the hallmark of the profession as a whole and distinguishes the professional officer. Furthermore, the military holds a monopoly on this particular expertise. No one else may both possess and apply it.

The second characteristic Huntington cites is social responsibility. The nature of military expertise imposes an obligation upon the military to execute its function not for selfish ends but only in the service of society. The military profession does not exist for self-interest, profit, or personal motives.

Corporateness, the final characteristic, means that there is a shared sense of organic unity and group consciousness which manifests itself in a particular professional organization. The organization formalizes, applies, and enforces the standards of professional competence. For the individual, membership in the organization is a criterion of professional status; laymen are excluded. In the case of the military, Huntington designates the officer corps as the professional organization. Not all officers are considered professionals in his view, however, since some lack functional competence in the peculiar military expertise of management of violence. Those only temporarily serving, with no thought of a military career, are only amateurs. Enlisted men, as a group, are considered tradesmen and are outside the professional corps, although many career soldiers may qualify for the higher status—most frequently those in the upper non-commissioned ranks.

Huntington's model is attractive in its consistency and logic, and it is true that the military does share in some measure characteristics of other professional groups such as law and medicine. But the analogy is insufficient to describe the military as a profession, or as an adequate basis for progress. The error is due to the attempt to find characteristics in the military which allow it to fall within a conventional definition of profession better fitted to other recognized groups. Rather than defining the military by its own distinguishing characteristics, it is interpreted in accordance with a socially standardized definition. This approach leads to the search for a particular expertise upon which the military can peg its professional status.

There are two basic objections to this approach. First, "management of violence" (or similar formulations for the same thing such as "the ordered application of force to the resolution of a social problem") is insufficient to describe what is actually required of the American military establishment in our contemporary global security commitments. Second, the military profession cannot be defined sufficiently in terms of any single functional expertise.

Military expertise is not a constant; it is contingent and relative. Military expertise will vary according to whatever is required of the profession to support the policies of the state. The range of possibilities includes a broad variety of skills and tasks encompassing not only the traditional tasks related to leadership in combat but many technical and managerial ones as well.

Within our defense establishment, the past decades have seen a great transformation in the skills required of the military. The widespread use of systems analysis and our mushrooming technology have created whole new dimensions of military expertise necessary for national security. Quite obviously, any attempt to decide who is a professional, based only upon the relationship of his occupational skill to management of violence or combat role, is arbitrary and too restricted. It also can be self-denying in terms of doing what is required by the country, if the military does not comprehend a broader role and develop the necessary skills as part of professional expertise. Combat expertise, of course, is the single most vital skill of the soldier, and one uniquely his to develop and use. Certainly it is both basic and essential to the value and effectiveness of the combat arms, and for the entire combat Army as described in Chapter 11. Hopefully, however, this would not lead to the exclusion of all other essential skills needed by the military, particularly in the support Army. As discussed in earlier chapters, a more sustainable, specialized, and capital-intensive Army will put a premium on a range of professional skills. Societal changes toward greater diversity reinforce the need to recognize greater diversity within the professional ranks. As Morris Janowitz points out in *The Professional Soldier,* there is a narrowing skill differential between military and civilian elites. The task now is to make appropriate adjustment in our thinking about the profession to take this into account.

The other two characteristics which Huntington cites —responsibility and corporateness—are indeed features of the military profession, although they are of importance independent of any combat-related expertise.

Huntington's model has been discussed at some length because it has come to dominate much of the thinking about the profession and illustrates the tendency toward narrowness, an urge to define the profession as unitary in origin rather than pluralistic. The effects of this can be unfortunate.

This has been at least a part of the reason for the tremendous pressures to reduce the length of the command tour. With relatively few commands available in comparison with the number of professional officers who "march to the sound of the guns," the competition becomes intense—as the Vietnam experience amply demonstrated. A broader concept of professionalism and a corresponding program of career development would avoid this.

A More Pluralistic Profession

We must construct a concept of professionalism for the military on a different basis than for other groups such as lawyers and doctors. The term itself has to mean something different in the military case.

The military profession can be properly defined only in

terms of both its purpose and the conditions placed upon the fulfillment of that purpose. The military exists only for the service of the state, regardless of the skills required or functions performed. As a profession the military does not condition this commitment, for in the words of Lt. Gen. Sir John Hackett, a distinguished British soldier-scholar, the contract for service includes an "unlimited liability clause," cited in Chapter 11 as vital to the combat Army as a whole.

The military's obligation of unconditional service to the lawful authority of the state is unique. There are, from time to time, changes in the nature of expertise required for this service. There may even be changes in the meaning of national security itself when viewed in terms of policies and programs. But these do not alter the basic character of the military profession. Many people outside the profession may have a self-imposed commitment to unconditional service to the state, but only the military possesses the obligation *collectively* as a defining characteristic. Certainly, in this respect, it is far different from any other profession.

The military's status as a profession, therefore, can be defined only in terms of its unique, unconditional obligation to serve the lawful authority of the state. It will develop whatever expertise is required to fulfill its unlimited contract for public service.

Obviously there is room here for all variety of dedicated individuals who possess needed skills. The profession does not have to be unitary. There is a hard core which must serve as a common denominator, however.

The officer cannot be a member of his profession without subscribing to the operating norms of his professional community as a whole. These norms are in fact a necessity for the success of the group in fulfilling its tasks. Without a collective sense of duty the military could not function and certainly could not be trusted. Military professionals must share a sense of duty to the nation. The professional officer must be an unconditional servant of state policy; he must have a deep normative sense of duty to do this. The rigorous demands made upon the profession by this sense of duty, and the tasks required of it, explain the premium placed upon other "soldierly" qualities. One cannot do his duty unless he has courage, selflessness, and integrity. The military profession must have these group values as a functional necessity.

A sense of duty is necessary, but not sufficient, for professional status. The person must have competence to perform the service required to fulfill his obligations as well. As described earlier, this may require one or more of a number of skills. Finally, he must be a member of the armed forces for an extended period of time. By joining the officer corps he makes his professional commitment and adopts the values of the military community as his own.

Professionalism is more than simply belonging to the officer corps. It is a status determined jointly by the officer and his government. Neither the state nor the officer corps will grant professional standing to the man who lacks the necessary competence or who will not agree to make an unconditional commitment to duty if he is in the combat Army. The unconditional quality of this commitment is signified by the career length and life of selfless sacrifice, ranging from Melville Goodwin's "genteel poverty" to the Gettysburg "last full measure of devotion."

Professionalism thus has both objective and subjective content. It is objective in that professional status is granted by the state if certain performance criteria are met by the officer. It is subjective in that the officer must feel a sense of duty to serve the lawful government "for the full distance," even at the risk of his life. Mentally, he does not condition this obligation.

Some may feel the denial of a single professional expertise akin to that of law or medicine is a self-inflicted wound. We would argue, on the contrary, that the acceptance of our broader concept of professionalism is essential to enable the

Army to respond to new conditions and to accept a more demanding role in national security policy. *As a profession of unlimited service, no skill which is necessary for the Army to fulfill its military obligation to the nation conflicts with the professional status of the officer.*

This concept of professionalism clearly applies to the military as we have come to view it in today's Army, and would likewise be sufficient without difficulty for the combat portion of a pluralistic Army. But the nature of a support Army would require a somewhat different mani-festation of professionalism. Obviously the officer who provides a non-combat specialty will probably never have to face up to "going the full distance" as may the infantry officer. And based upon the functional requirements of the Army, his service may not even be required on a continuous basis. What then defines his professionalism? To answer this, we must go back to the basic purpose of the military itself. The military exists only to perform a service to the state of which it is a creature. No elements of it, combat or support, can be in business independently. Therefore, all members of the organization must be required to place some value upon the higher goals of the military if they are to be accorded professional status. Within the support Army, subordination to a higher goal would be represented by a choice between monetary compensation in return for limited obligated service, on the one hand, and professional compensation to include career benefits in return for longer term commit-ment, largely on the government's terms, on the other hand.

Educational development might serve to illustrate the distinction. The "professional" member of the support Army might leave the uniformed service to attend graduate civil schooling. But he would do so at the expense of the government and with a commitment to repay the government in service at a later time. Retirement benefits would eventually compensate his obligation. The non-professional specialist, on the other hand, could also leave active service to receive graduate education, but would do so without obligation to return to service and without financial assistance. But during his stay on active service he might well be paid somewhat more than his professional counterpart to compensate for the absence of tenure.

Essentially we accept that the core professional attribute for both combat and support Army personnel is commitment to the service of the state through the military institution. Simultaneously we acknowledge that the attribute of service can carry different forms in a diverse pluralistic Army.

Ethos of Service—The Meaning of Duty

A more pluralistic profession raises the question of diversity with regard to motivations of different type professionals within a single professional organization. As discussed earlier, all must share a commitment of duty. But widely varying conditions of service, career patterns, educational backgrounds, and even life styles mean that in everyday affairs the meaning of duty will and must inevitably take appropriately different forms.

We are familiar with the traditional forms usually measured against the absolute norm of combat and "putting our life on the line." This will continue as an important ethical model. As in the past the combat officers of the Army will be given constant reminders of this standard both in their educational development and as they undergo rigorous and demanding field training which keeps the organization attuned to a battlefield psychology.

Support Army officers will also be exposed to this concept of duty in their professional education; however, we must develop an outlook which is more relevant to their everyday concern. The professional within the support Army will be distinguished from his peers by his approach to his responsibilities. In contrast to the non-professional, he will have an abiding "proprietary interest" in the enhancement of the organization as opposed to advancement of his own particular interests.

An analogy to business might be appropriate here. A "member of the firm" is concerned with the long-term interests of the organization and will make short-term personal sacrifices to advance these interests. He interprets rules and regulations from the standpoint of how they contribute to the well-being of the organization as a whole rather than an arbitrary set of rules laid down to inhibit individual behavior. This latter approach might well characterize the attitude of an "in-and-outer" in a business firm. The professional officer in the support Army will in his outlook be a "member of the firm." The Army will have first claim on his interests. He will share the goals of the Army in fulfilling the spirit of the regulations.

This ethos must be fostered by initially exposing the officer to the overall goals and purposes of the organization and his place in it—as is now done generally by focusing on the combat Army, assuming that the model is suitable for the Army as a whole. But the sense of duty of the professional in the support Army will require continued reinforcement as he progresses in responsibility. In contrast to the non-professional, he must be given recognition that he is a "member of the firm" by preferential assignments and opportunities for broadening experiences.

Enhancing Individualism

The profession requires constructive initiative. There is a perennial dilemma in attempting to foster innovative thought and encourage individuals to stand on principle, even if it is unpopular or at odds with established opinion. On the one hand, large organizations ossify if individualism is stifled. But on the other hand, individualism can be destructive of an organization if taken to an extreme.

Therefore, in asking for individual strength of conviction and willingness to "stand up and be counted," we condition this with several caveats. First we seek a balance—order and diversity in harmony. We do not seek initiative at the price of the destruction of essential discipline. Secondly, we seek initiative not in order to fulfill individual psychic needs for recognition but to serve the broader interests of the organization. This leads to a third and final condition: we wish to foster initiative from those whose values and abilities complement and support the longer term interests of the Army.

This last point may very well mean that in effect true freedom to dissent is legitimate only for a minority grouping within the organization which by some means has been identified as constructive and basically loyal, even if at times disconcerting. The distinction is the difference between a professional who will risk his own career for the betterment of the organization and one who, while perhaps attempting to appear to be similarly motivated, in fact either does not value the organization's survival or would subordinate it to his own ends or psychic needs.

Within these three important constraints, the Army must carefully insure that it foster a forthright and independent-minded core of professionals. It is not that the officer corps consists of conformists; it does not. But the profession must constantly attempt to provide incentives to demonstrate distinctive excellence and to do more than that which the system has identified as adequate. Any tendency to maintain a convenient myth of professionalism which shies from paying the price of enforcing the rigorous standards of competition which would make professional status truly meaningful must be avoided at all costs.

To take but one aspect of this issue—our schooling system. The low percentage of failure at our Army officer schools may imply that the system is not designed to stimulate sufficiently productive competition among professionals.

And one of the implications of this is that there may be little or no overt incentive for accepting responsibility for making critical judgments about officer standards. To flunk out an officer is painful and difficult. It is much easier to accept a minimum standard and permit all to stay than it is to acknowledge difference in ability and motivation.

A profession whose stock in trade is the ability to make hard life-and-death decisions in situations of great stress must not shy from hard decisions concerning professional education. We think that the profession would benefit from enforcement of more rigorous professional standards. This is the means by which we would attempt to improve the conditions for encouraging responsible individualism within the ranks of the career officer corps.

Much of our concern about stimulating greater individual initiative expressed above could also be described as the case against equity—a common concern of large organizations, that all receive equal treatment. Let there be no mistake. All should be treated *fairly;* but not all can or should be treated *equally.* We believe that individual distinctive excellence should be more explicitly encouraged by the Army.

FROM THEORY INTO PRACTICE: NEW DIRECTIONS

Translating a concept of pluralistic professionalism into practice requires substantial initiatives in several key areas. These are officer career management (which is now being addressed by the Army); officer education; and officer recruitment and retention policy.

Officer Career Patterns

At the present time, the Army is grappling with the need to move toward more pluralistic and specialized patterns of career development for officers, which will serve the needs of the service for diverse contributions, and the needs of the individual for a meaningful career.

This is the purpose behind the recently publicized Officer Personnel Management System (OPMS). OPMS proposes a substantial modification in officer career management, primarily through heavier emphasis on specialization. In other words, the Army is re-examining the essence of military professionalism.

Now being seriously considered, the new system would do three things. It requires all officers to develop both a primary and secondary specialty early in his career; it makes command a "specialty" open only to a few officers, thereby sharply limiting those in competition for command positions; and it provides far greater opportunities for advancement to the rank of general officer via a variety of non-command specialty (support Army) routes. Full implementation will of course take several years to accomplish.

This would be a substantial departure from the current system which has reflected the self-image of a unitary "management of violence" career force. In order to maintain this image, while yet encompassing a broad array of different functions within the professional officer corps, the career system has traditionally defined "specialist" as very narrow indeed, including distinctly "non-military" functions such as medicine and religion. All other skills related to "management of violence" were included under the umbrella of "generalist." In other words, the contributions of the great majority of officers have been considered to be sufficiently similar to allow for a common career pattern for all but a few. OPMS would not just tolerate but rather reward the development of individual skills.

We consider the goals of OPMS highly desirable for evolution to the professional officer corps we consider necessary for the future. We support its rapid implementation.

Officer Education

As we have discussed above, the Army's educational system—a crucial aspect of military professionalism—will require substantial revision to support a more specialized officer corps and a more pluralistic Army. First and most basic, the Army should encourage competition within the Army school system by a combination of curriculum and faculty reform. The curriculum must both educate (requires exercise of logic) rather than train (requires assimilation of doctrine and proven technique) and it must explicitly measure achievement in the academic environment to include dismissing those not meeting minimum standards.

Second, the educational system should be changed to develop distinct patterns for the combat Army, on the one hand, as compared to the support Army, on the other. The thrust of the change would have the command specialist generally operate within the combat Army system, while most other specialists would follow the educational pattern within the support Army.

The educational system within the combat Army would change little. The combat arms employment schools, Command and General Staff College and War College, would be maintained with modest changes to improve understanding of current social problems and to increase the professional content. Civilian graduate education should be retained as much for the integrative effects of exposure to civilian elite groups as for the academic discipline. It should be possible, however, to focus on those disciplines which are most relevant to the combat Army.

The support Army would rely heavily on educational and training techniques developed by civilian industry. Technical service schools and an Administrative/Logistics College equivalent to the Command and General Staff College should provide sufficient professional content. These should be complemented with extensive graduate schooling in technical areas for officers and use of civilian skill improvement centers for NCOs. All officers would expect continuing upgrading of their technical skills throughout their term of service.

Officer Recruitment and Retention

Once the concept of a more pluralistic profession is accepted, it should be possible also to initiate more diversified patterns of officer recruitment and retention.

Recruitment of officers for the combat Army would generally follow currently established patterns. Entry would be at the lowest rank, with a required minimum age which is quite young. Leadership potential, character, and general intelligence would be basic criteria. For the support Army, more weight would be given to the particular skills of the officers. For a range of specialties, entry into commissioned service might be much later in life and at a higher grade than would be the case for combat arms officers. The background required of the officer upon entry would be that necessary for his specialty rather than for an increasingly responsible role in leading others.

Promotion and retention policies would also vary. Promotion policy would favor the combat officers both as an incentive to service and due to the physical demands of leadership of combat forces. Combat Army leaders would face accelerated promotion and force out. The system should permit most officers to command companies from about age 25 to 30, battalions from 30 to 35, and brigades from 35 to 40. General officers should be required to retire at age 50 unless selected for promotion to lieutenant general by that age.

The support Army would have very liberal promotion policies permitting captains or majors at age 40 to 45. Colonels would be permitted to remain on active service until age 60. More rapid promotion would be possible but exceptional. The basic attraction of service in the support Army is the satisfaction of public service through continued improvement in technical competence in a stable, financially secure environment.

Chapter 14

PROFESSIONAL COMPETENCE AND INTEGRITY

The quality of the reputation of the military profession and particularly the Army is a crucial element in military capability. It influences the nature and attributes of the men and women we attract and retain, and it determines the weight that our counsel is accorded in national security decision-making. Most crucially, it deeply affects the attitudes and abilities of the men whose lives are entrusted to our leadership in difficult, dangerous situations.

The professional standard is rigorous. Our reputation must be one of dedicated service, professional competence, personal integrity, and absolute honor. In the eyes of many, we as a group fail to meet that high standard today, either to ourselves or to both trusting and skeptical outsiders. There are no short cuts, no selling gimmicks that need be stressed. To improve our reputation we must continue to do better even if fairly drastic remedial action is required. Honest improvement evident within the profession will reflect itself in improved public appreciation.

We will discuss policies which could enhance the credibility of the military profession. However, to develop the solutions, we must appreciate several of the sources of our recent malaise—some but not all of which center on Vietnam.

[233]

Particularly important sources are widespread public criticism, general difficulties caused by the method of raising forces for Vietnam, questionable practices which had evolved since World War II but which became manifest in Vietnam, and changing characteristics of youth in modern post-industrial America.

Public criticism of the Army owes much of its stridency to an unhappy convergence of events. There has been extensive deliberate and inadvertent defamation stimulated by honest and well-meaning supporters of competing resource demands. A number of dedicated Americans believe that a reduced external threat should permit increased resources to be allocated to pressing domestic needs—improved education, alleviation of inner-city ills, and environmental improvement. The Urban Coalition's *Counterbudget* is an example of this sentiment. It is reasonable to expect that management errors such as weapons systems cost overruns will be used to dramatize the inefficient use of funds. The Nye Committee excelled in this form of public inquiry prior to World War II. Such free competition of ideas is a part of the public dialogue which strengthens our democracy.

Not all criticism has been responsible, however, but unfortunately, anti-military propagandists have been aided by gross Army errors. My Lai, the Service Clubs scandal, and the affair concerning the Army's former Provost Marshal General are shocking failures of integrity which not only the critical propagandist but also the quiet but observant Middle American notes. There is no acceptable excuse. Any profession charged with the responsibilities of "unlimited liability" must have checks and balances to prevent or quickly stop such conduct. These restraints operated imperfectly at times during the Vietnam period.

The publicity afforded evident errors has been augmented by serious criticism of the conduct of the war in Vietnam from within the service. In a curious, confusing amalgam of perceptive criticism and self-serving commentary, former officers have provided the semblance of professional expertise to the critical press.

Lastly there has been the normal public disillusionment after a lengthy war, perhaps stimulated by intensive TV coverage and comment. It has been present after Vietnam as it was after World War II and Korea. All of the conflict zones between the individual and a disciplined military society have been probed regularly—military justice, discipline, and AWOL, with the new Vietnam elements of drugs and race. These were in many cases valid criticisms. They are discomfiting to the military, but they reflect healthy public and Congressional concern which is an integral part of service in a democracy.

Each of the sources of criticism is serious, but taken individually none is disabling. Combined as they have been in the recent past, however, they can be debilitating. They may be sufficient to cause the average American to question the basic competence and integrity of his Army. If the citizen ever questions to the point that he is unwilling to freely permit his son to serve, the Army and the nation are in serious straits. For the Army is a mass organization, and its strengths derive from the support of the society it serves. It will no longer be effective if the bulk of society ever concludes that the Army's purposes or values are at odds with those required of a servant of the nation.

Some questioning of the Army resulted from the complex nature of the war in Vietnam. It has been an extraordinarily difficult war, conducted successfully without expected mobilization by a superb capital-intensive force, in an undeveloped area against a personnel-intensive enemy for non-military objectives. The Army can justifiably be proud of the job it did in terms of the principal military tasks it was assigned.

Unfortunately, some long-term costs of the decision not to mobilize are now becoming evident in such manner as to bring into question the competence of the Army. Unable to call up significant numbers of reserve personnel, we were required to rapidly integrate many officers. Furthermore, we had to create support units to fill the void of non-mobilization. Today, relying again on mobilization for planning purposes, many of these skills are surplus. As a result, we have had many superbly skilled individuals assigned to tasks for which they are not trained or are over-trained.

Less obvious but more crucial in the long run, we adjusted our school system to focus on preparation for the immediate problem of Vietnam. Schools, doctrine, and research/development resources were diverted from preparation for mid-intensity conflict. They are now being redirected, but there is a serious transitional educational/training gap in many young officers and NCOs.

Added to the inevitable impact on our competence of the crash effort to mobilize from within for Vietnam, there has been the effect of a number of questionable practices which had evolved during World War II and Korea and which came to a head in Vietnam.

The first "malpractice" reflects the inevitable expansion of science and technology to the battlefield. Vietnam is the first war where technology in the form of greatly improved transportation (the helicopter) and communications has radically transformed the command and control of tactical units. The comforting traditional necessity and practice of the chain of command was set aside with often poor results. In many cases, good small unit commanders were beseiged by excellent, dynamic, aggressive higher commanders anxious to influence the action from a helicopter vantage point. Intermediate commanders were denied the responsibility, the challenge, and the pleasure of command by ever-present, often overweening higher commanders.

Conversely, the helicopter permitted poor commanders to command the infantry soldier facing danger directly from the cool, distant safety of an orbiting helicopter, sallying forth at comfortable intervals from his base camp. Neither of these images is wholly fair—they are, however, stereotypes which are real and which must be overcome for they are corrosive images in the Army consciousness.

A second understandable but questionable practice is the "11B syndrome" derived from the lack of public support for the war. (11B being the MOS which identifies the basic infantry rifleman.) The 11B syndrome manifested itself in two ways—extravagant use of combat support and extremely high levels of combat service support. Knowing the inequities of the draft, the difficulties of jungle terrain, the skill of the Viet Cong infantryman, and the general availability of plentiful combat support resources—a legacy of Korea—many commanders demanded more and more artillery and air power in order to reduce casualty rates. Understandable in itself, this attitude of over-insurance by extravagant use of resources became the crutch for the poor commander. A disturbing legacy of extensive combat support requirements has been established beyond the legitimate and necessary needs of capital intensification.

The other element of the 11B syndrome is the extraordinarily high level of combat service support. The concept is understandable—do all that we can to make the life style of the draftee infantryman comparable to his deferred compatriot back in the United States. The result—plush base camps, officer and NCO clubs, air conditioning, and so on—very little of which was available to the 11B. Vietnam accustomed many in the Army to a level of living which is not only beyond the will and means of America but which will be positively detrimental if it carries over to mid-intensity conflict. Further, it created a dangerous rift between the volunteer regular "lifer" and the young draftee which will haunt the Army through the attitudes of the embittered veteran.

A third questionable practice was spawned generally in Europe as a result of the resource priority afforded to Vietnam. U.S. Army Europe was knowingly drawn down to support the war in Vietnam. Unfortunately, standards were not noticeably reduced as resources dried up—units with a handful of officers and rapidly rotating personnel were ostensibly evaluated by the same standards which applied to the pre-Vietnam 7th Army. The result was an intolerable stretching of the reporting honesty and integrity of the junior officer. The can-do attitude in the face of limited resources as it has been frequently reflected in overly optimistic charts —be they training proficiency or kill rates—must not be allowed to infect the Army.

Another challenge to the Army is the incorporation of modern management techniques into a large organization responsible for a broad range of dissimilar activities. Many have substituted the security of complex charts and indicators of success for the personal intuitive judgments of interpersonal contact. In the face of acknowledged complexity, many have taken refuge in the haven of statistics. The distortions which such techniques can present to higher authority are as relevant and dangerous to the subordinate commander today as they have been in the past.

The third disturbing but unavoidable characteristic of our modern society is the continuing intensive scrutiny by media. The compression of time and the trauma of color TV in the living room with the instant portrayal and interpretation erase the old buffers of time and of intervening subsequent events in war. We must expect and accept an unblinking public eye on all that we do. We will not always be right; we will never know all of the facts; we must, however, be honest and forthright in our actions, be they right or misguided. With our media, today and tomorrow, the penalty for evasiveness will be not only certain failure but erosion of confidence in the credibility of the profession.

The current public and to some extent self-image of the Army is an amalgam of the complex sources indicated above. In the aggregate, the image is of a generally well-meaning but somewhat incompetent, complacent, and unresponsive organization. The intellectual would probably see it as an overgrown bureaucracy tending to be in business for itself. These images will be decreased only by positive actions which are wholly credible to the officers and men of the Army.

NEW DIRECTIONS

There are no certain comprehensive "solutions" to the promotion of "credibility." One has to select the key areas, then hope that there are sufficient understandable, supportable responsive decision rules which can be implemented across the great diversity of situations which is the Army. Certain of these have been touched on earlier. These issues of leadership and competence are basic to every aspect of the Army. Therefore, even at the risk of some repetition, several areas for decision guidance are stated below to bring these related issues together and to lend emphasis to the importance we attach to professional credibility. These seem to bear promise as ways to improve the reality and image of Army competence and readiness.

(1) *Reduce the peacetime chain of command:* The chain of command should be based upon loci of authority and responsibility both to allocate time, personnel, and money and to direct the mission. In other words, he who assigns the mission must control or be able to responsibly influence the allocation of all resources for the accomplishment of the mission. Here we may be able to turn current management practices and capabilities to productive use. The centralization of resource allocation stimulated by sophisticated automatic data processing (ADP) may permit a major pruning of the chain of command in peacetime. Perhaps every other headquarters in current chains of command could be eliminated—with traditional tactical headquarters reconstituted solely for conduct of major field exercises. If we

err, the error should be in overreduction. Parkinson's Law will act continuously to create or enlarge headquarters.

(2) *Maintain divisions and brigades at full TOE strength:* Establish manning guidance to ensure that divisions or brigades are maintained at full strength and to ensure that there is no more than a thirty-five percent personnel turnover per year. Arbitrary decision guidance for force structure planning which reflects this emphasis would ensure that there are sufficient men in units to properly train on crew-served equipment and that personnel are in a unit long enough to develop pride, job satisfaction, and sense of unit identity. This policy is explicit recognition of the need for quality rather than quantity of units. The Army has maintained traditionally understrength units both for strategic "presence" and as a demonstrable claimant for acquiring new resources. This deliberate anemia creates an impossible situation at the unit level. Undesirable but feasible in the past, the loss of job satisfaction which it creates cannot continue in a volunteer environment.

(3) *Develop management practices to stimulate individual acceptance of responsibility and personal integrity:* The Army must devise techniques to stimulate the development of strong individualists. While institutions cannot legislate morality, they can create an environment which fosters rather than inhibits individual development. For example, in an earlier chapter we proposed new guidance on the use of unit time—a standard of challenging demanding training required to develop genuinely ready units rather than the commonplace two honest days of training "compressed" into five days of mediocre time consumption. Such policies stimulate the moral courage required of young commanders to use time effectively. Other incentives would be peer ratings of former unit or job associates with strong emphasis on individualism and independent problem solving or permitting each officer or NCO to have ten to twenty percent of his efficiency reports disregarded for personnel actions. The point is to redesign management practices to reward individualism not conformity.

(4) *Ensure that our units are led by our most capable leaders:* The most crucial actions are underway now within the provisions of

OPMS discussed in Chapter 13. That is, selection of the most suitable officers for command and the stabilization of command tours so that the most qualified commanders can develop and train a unit. To supplement this, some procedure should be developed so that every officer commissioned in the combat arms spends a period of service in the enlisted ranks. For example, ROTC and U.S. Military Academy cadets might serve as infantry privates in line units during one or more of their summer training periods. The purpose of this policy would be to ensure that young officers understand the fears, motivations, abilities, and problems of enlisted soldiers and the enlisted chain of command. To maintain this awareness, we should consider policies whereby selected combat arms officers would be encouraged to visit with a field unit each year.

(5) *Equalize the physical amenities provided to married personnel —particularly family service and quarters facilities:* The Army is no democracy and there should be special amenities associated with senior grade and experience. There should, however, be equity in provision of the basic requirements of life—food and shelter in particular—across the Army ranks. Today, the term "family Army" must apply to all soldiers, and each grade should share overseas service equally. The inequities of service in Europe, for example, are great. Quarters are not provided to all married personnel. Present dependents facilities in Europe create an undesirable differentiation of life style within supposedly highly ready combat units. To some it is an extension of the disturbing life style differential between the infantry draftee and the base camp "lifer" in Vietnam. The married NCO and officer return to their families each evening—in some cases this can amount to abdicating responsibilities to a "counter chain of command" dominated by race or drugs. The young soldier alone in a foreign culture or trying to start family life in marginal, substandard local housing must not be left to his own devices when he most needs help. This strikes at the basis of professional integrity and credibility and cannot be tolerated.

(6) *Develop standards and techniques for continuing officer evaluation:* Another ingredient of improved leadership would be to establish a more vigorous officer evaluation system. We tend to

treat our officer corps as a cozy club. Once commissioned, there are few vigorous professional examinations of the officer, yet the NCO faces numerous proficiency exams. The officer should be capable of demonstrating branch proficiency or career specialty frequently as do aviators now by annual exam. Further, officers at selected grades should be subject to evaluation by their subordinates. In sum there are many procedural variations; the crucial element is that the officer be expected to "lay it on the line" and demonstrate his proficiency to his men more frequently—similar to the requirements of the soldier.

(7) *Reduce the numbers of serving officers:* While it is probably undesirable to insist that no officer or NCO work for another of the same grade, it does appear feasible and desirable to reduce the numbers of 0-5, 0-6, and general officers by a sizeable percentage. Parallel arbitrary reductions should be made on the Army General Staff and its operating agencies and the major operating commands in CONUS. Many will argue that the job cannot be done at reduced levels. While that may be a valid case, many would argue that competent, job-satisfying work is not being done today, and as a result we are accomplishing less than we think we are. The size of a staff is a poor guide to its worth or effectiveness.

Some of the medicine prescribed above is stiff. Some of it may, upon analysis, be infeasible. But some current problems require stark solutions. The "revival" of values we propose will not be easy. In concluding, it is therefore appropriate to look once more to the enduring basis of the military profession, to one other value upon which it is founded —personal integrity.

Despite frequent inferences to the contrary, military professionalism does not require the abdication of moral responsibility. It does require as a practical matter that a person's moral judgments be reconciled with service to the state if he is to serve it in a professional capacity. This can be determined only by the person himself. The profession itself, as a creature of the state, is a legal abstraction and as such cannot take a moral stand. The individual cannot avoid it.

The U.S. commissioning oath is an unlimited liability contract that obliges the officer to defend the Constitution against all enemies. There is no escape clause, since military professionalism denies the officer the right as a soldier to determine who the enemy is or what the Constitution is. These decisions are left to the civil institutions. The soldier does not even have the right to be consulted. He may be asked to advise—it is his function; but he must consent—it is his professional duty. Any departure from this discipline is a denial of the professional trust.

The officer cannot, simultaneously in his capacity as a military professional, act as a private citizen freely exercising his Constitutional rights and also exercise personal moral choice with regard to national policy requiring military execution. Yet his basic integrity and humane society both forbid the officer to evade personal moral responsibility for his acts. Thus, there is a dilemma and a risk in being a military professional. The demands of duty and morality are both based on absolutes. No formula can solve this inherent conflict, because to the military professional, duty itself must be one of his moral values.

The claims of moral conscience cannot be denied, even if silenced by rationalization; and personal moral responsibility is inescapable in civilized society, regardless of the consequences. In the ethics of military professionalism, devotion to duty is paramount, the core of honorable service to the country. But the human being who wears the uniform must live within his conscience's moral universe. Hopefully, the demands of duty and conscience can be reconciled; if not, then choices must be made. However, in cases of conflict, a choice in favor of either duty or morality will not excuse a person from the consequences of offending against the responsibilities of the other alternative. The dilemma is uncompromising.

This fundamental fact was seen and expressed clearly by a soldier who paid dearly for maintaining his integrity and honesty: General Ludwig Beck, chief of staff of the German Army until purged by Chancellor Adolf Hitler. General Beck wrote in 1938: "History will indict the highest leaders of the Wehrmacht with blood-guilt if they do not act in accordance with expert and statesmanlike knowledge and assurance. Their duty of soldierly obedience finds its limit when their knowledge, conscience and responsibility forbid the execution of an order." It has been the world's tragedy that, unlike General Beck, the majority of his fellow officers could feel justified in living up to a concept of professionalism which excused the soldier from personal responsibility. They rationalized their duty as basically to the Army itself. The German officer corps' concept of professionalism led it to abdicate personal moral responsibility and to shift the burden of moral choice to the profession itself as a corporate body. But the corporate military institution itself cannot make moral judgments of state policy. Rather, the military is both the creation and the instrument of state policy, and subject to the state's authority.

The West Point motto, "Duty, Honor, Country," succinctly states the essential characteristics of military professionalism. The soldier's first loyalty is to his country, whose values and purposes he has solemnly sworn to uphold. The soldier's obligation to do his duty in the service of the state is uncompromising and has no reservations. His honor is the moral measure of duty faithfully performed, even at the risk of death, in the service of his country.

The basic obligation of the professional soldier is therefore to *act* in accordance with these precepts. How he interprets these in the light of particular circumstances and how he chooses to act come to be determined ultimately by individual integrity. Personal integrity is thus the crucial, enduring basis of the military profession—the rock upon which it must be founded. Legal and procedural safeguards against lack of integrity will always be necessary, but they will never be sufficient.

The substantial changes suggested in this book assume that this central feature of the profession, integrity, will enable the Army to make whatever difficult choices are necessary in the interests of adjusting to new circumstances.

We are optimistic as to the outcome.

AFTERWORD

Almost a year has passed since the basic manuscript for this book was prepared. This passage of time has afforded us the opportunity to gain additional perspective both as to the nature of the various challenges facing the Army and the responses which have been developed by the service.

A number of innovative actions have been taken. There has been a fundamental reorganization of the Army within the United States which has resulted in a tangible reduction in support overhead and a serious addressal of the problems of reserve readiness. The Modern Volunteer Army program has been developed to attract accessions and the Volunteer Army (VOLAR) experiment conducted to evaluate the effect of different life style measures. The Officer Personnel Management Systems study (OPMS) has evolved to a point that it offers the prospect of paced yet responsible recognition of the need for officer specialization. While we do not agree with the thrust of all of the innovations, particularly some of those associated with VOLAR, we believe that they are a very healthy sign of the Army's ability to take a hard look at itself.

There has been quiet, steady progress in a number of key areas. We are profoundly encouraged by the emphasis which has been placed upon decentralization of authority to local leadership. Aggressive recruiting appears to be providing adequate numbers of suitably qualified young men and women. A concentrated effort is being made to improve the quality of training. The local unit is being better supported with personnel resources. Most importantly, the Army has buckled down to the task of rebuilding a skilled, tough, proud, disciplined Ready Army.

We would caution students of the military profession that they need to examine closely their data concerning Army characteristics and motivations. The stereotypes of the last several years of the Vietnam conflict may not be applicable to the present, for the Army has changed profoundly in this period with the impact of the end of the war and volunteer accessions. It will change again as the impact of volunteer status expands.

In sum, we are very encouraged by what we have seen. There is much yet to be done, but the Army is unquestionably on the right course.

Z.B.B. and F.J.B.
Alexandria, Virginia
March 1973

WORKS CITED

BRADFORD, Z. B. and J. N. MURPHY (1969) "A new look at the military profession." Army, February.

FALL, B. (1964) *Street Without Joy*. Harrisburg, Pa.: Stackpole.

HACKWORTH, D. H. (1968) *A Distant Challenge*. Birmingham, Ala.: Birmingham.

HUNTINGTON, S. P. (1957) *The Soldier and the State: The Theory and Politics of Civil Military Relations*. Cambridge, Mass.: Harvard Univ.

JANOWITZ, M. (1960) *The Professional Soldier: A Social and Political Portrait*. New York: Free Press.

MOSKOS, C. C., Jr. (1971) "The emergent military: civilianized, traditional or pluralistic?" Presented to the American Political Science Association Annual Meeting.

YARMOLINSKY, A. (1971) *The Military Establishment: Its Impact on American Society*. Scranton, Pa.: Harper.

ABOUT THE AUTHORS

LTC FREDERIC J. BROWN is presently assigned to the 101st Airborne Division (Airmobile). He was commissioned in 1956 from the U.S. Military Academy, was an Olmsted Scholar at the Graduate Institute of International Studies, Geneva, Switzerland in 1963, and holds a Ph.D. in international relations. He completed the National War College in 1972.

His troop assignments include command of a Tank Company in Germany; operations officer of a Mechanized Infantry Battalion in Vietnam and command of the 1st Squadron, 4th Cavalry, 1st Infantry Division, in Vietnam.

Staff assignments include Division G-3 Plans and Division G-3 in Vietnam; service on the Joint Staff, Office Joint Chiefs of Staff and with the Office, Coordinator of Army Studies, Office of the Assistant Vice Chief of Staff, Washington, D.C.

In the latter capacity, he was involved in the conceptual development of the Modern Volunteer Army/VOLAR program and the Officer Personnel Management System. Most recently he has served as the Military Assistant to the Deputy Assistant to the President for National Security Affairs and Special Assistant to the Vice Chief of Staff, United States Army. In this capacity he has been associated with the development and execution of U.S. national security policy with respect to Southeast Asia.

LTC ZEB B. BRADFORD, JR. is presently assigned to the U.S. Army Infantry School, Ft. Benning, Ga. He was commissioned in 1956 from the U.S. Military Academy, and is a graduate of the U.S. Army Command and General Staff College and the Army War College. He holds a Master of Public Administration from Harvard (1964), and was an Assistant Professor of Social Science at the U.S. Military Academy. He was the first military officer selected as a Fellow of the Woodrow Wilson International Center for Scholars, Washington, D.C.

His troop assignments include command of an Infantry Company in Germany, service in the Ranger Department of the Army Infantry School, Operations Officer of an Infantry Battalion of the 9th Division in Vietnam, and command of an Infantry Battalion of the 2nd Division in Korea.

Staff assignments include Division G-3 Plans in Vietnam, Aide and Executive Officer to General Creighton W. Abrams in Vietnam, and service in the Office of the Assistant Vice Chief of Staff, Washington, D.C. While in the latter capacity he was deeply involved in Army strategic planning, resource management, and in developing policy initiatives for the Chief of Staff, U.S. Army.

INDEX

Anti-Ballistic Missile (ABM), 93, 153.
Active forces–Ready Army concepts, 158-159.
Adjutant General Corps–in Pluralistic Army, 194.
Advanced Attack Helicopter (AAH), selective procurement 134, 145; requirement in Europe, 118.
Air Force, general war capabilities, 93; in coalition support, 96; in contingencies, Korea, 94; Mid-East, 95; importance in Vietnam, 58-59, 68; airlift, in coalition support, 96; in improved training, 107; air superiority and helicopter operations, 68; assimilation, 132.
Airmobility; Airmobile Divison, 85; techniques in Vietnam, 58-59, 62-63; air cavalry, 143; training simulations, 116. See also doctrine, helicopters, Vietnam.
Allies, assistance requirements, 141; survivability assumptions, 90; dependence, 103-104; cooperation, 124; Ready Army, 153. See also coalition security.
Armor, Armored Division, 85; role in Vietnam, 61-62; in contingency operations, Korea, 94; Mid-East, 95; applicability for Asian allies, 126; support requirements, 137; assimilation, 133; armored cavalry 143; in Pluralistic Army, 194. See also capital intensification, contingency, Ready Army.
Army, reliance on other services, 68; capabilities for general war, 93; and guerrilla wars, 64; in coalition support, 96, 122; in resources control contingency, 95; the Ready Army, 83-84; manpower employment, 130; philosophical issues, 74, 170-171, 173, 176, 192, 200-201, 203, 235; acquisition policy, 118. See also Combat Army, Ready Army, Support Army.
Assimilation, 103, 133; of new weapons, 171; and conceptual change, 132.

Authoritarian, nature of Army, 179; discipline patterns, 196. See also discipline values.

Basic training, World War II, 155; Pluralistic Army, 200.
Battalion, in Ready Army, 85; combat/support ratio, 136; accelerated mobilization training, 156.
Budget, effect on volunteer status, 43; constraint to ground power, 23. 45; pressures, 46; projections, 131; focus on resources, 169. See also force structure, guidelines, logistics, manpower, Research and Development, Ready Army.

Cadre, in World War II, 155; in Ready Army, 154, 156, 159; support mobilization, 116-117. See also mobilization, reserves.
Capability, for coalition security, 125-126; for guerrilla war, 65; effect of Vietnam, 69; derived from NATO, 100; of Ready Army, 150. 153. See also contingency, force structure, Ready Army.
Capital intensification, 43, 55-56, 66 68, 127, 129, 130, 133-135, 139. 237; application in Vietnam, 59, 62; and Ready Army, 83; new directions, 141; influence of technological change, 133; problems of volunteer force, 131; demands on professionalism, 221; application to training, 117, 156, 163-164.
Coalition security, 23-24, 31-34 66-67, 84, 91, 99, 112-113, 119 122-123, 125, 158, 187; characteristics, 110; and Ready Army, 165; scenarios, 93; support for contingency operations, 97; impact on force development, 79; on Reserves, 109; resource costs, 148, costing assumptions, 150. See also ground forces, strategy.
Cobra-TOW, 118, 133.
Cold War, 21-22, 24; new assumptions, 31-32; contingencies, 81, 122. See also containment.